FLORIDA'S CLERKS OF THE CIRCUIT COURT

THEIR HISTORY AND EXPERIENCES

William Warren Rogers

and

Canter Brown, Jr.

William Warren Rogers (signature)

Sentry Press

Tallahassee, Florida

FLORIDA'S CLERKS OF THE CIRCUIT COURT
Their History and Experiences
© 1996 William Warren Rogers and Canter Brown, Jr.
ISBN 1-889574-00-7

All rights reserved. Printed in the United States of America. No part of this publication may be reproduced, stored in a retrieval system or transmitted in any form or by any means, electronic, mechanical, photocopying, recording or otherwise without the written permission of the publisher, except by a reviewer, who may quote brief passages for a review. All inquiries should be directed to Sentry Press, 424 East Call Street, Tallahassee, FL 32301.

"...the courthouse bell, the country courthouse, shaped life and destiny through America....and it was America as well with her unspoken prophecies, her unfound language, her unuttered song, and just for all these reasons it was for us all our own America, with all her horror, beauty, tenderness, and terror, with all we know of her that never has been proved, that never yet was uttered—the only one we know, the only one there is."
From Thomas Wolfe, "The Bell Remembered," in *The Years Beyond* (1935).

TABLE OF CONTENTS

Introduction..vii

Acknowledgments... ix

1. Beginnings.. 1

2. The Territorial Years, 1821-1845.. 5

3. The Constitution of 1838-1839, Statehood, and the Clerks....................................... 19

4. Courthouses, Trials, Tribulations, and Personalities... 27

5. Through the Civil War.. 41

6. Reconstruction and Redemption.. 51

7. Responsibilities Fulfilled--And the Future.. 65

8. Tradition and Diversity: Facing the Challenges of the Modern Era 79

9. Strength Through Unity... 91

Endnotes.. 99

Bibliography...106

Index..113

PHOTO ILLUSTRATIONS
(to be found following page 54)

Andrew Jackson

The Spanish Provost Guard House

Robert Meacham

Samuel Pasco

INTRODUCTION

This study has been underwritten by the Florida Association of Court Clerks and Comptrollers. Executive Director Roger Alderman and the Association's board of directors, noting the unavailability of any historical study of Florida's circuit clerks, commissioned the authors to write one. As historians and students of Florida and southern history, we welcomed the opportunity to research and write about one of the key historical figures in local government.

As Alderman and numerous clerks explained to us, the constitutional office of clerk serves the public in many capacities, not the least being its part in helping to maintain the checks and balances of government. Although frequently used by Floridians, it is little known to them. The clerk is an important player in executive and judicial matters who has been on the scene since Florida became a territory in the 1820s. A citizen who obtains a marriage license or records a real estate transaction deals with the clerk's office, and there are countless other points of contact between the clerk, his or her staff, and the public. Although the clerk is popularly elected every four years, voters do not consider the office "political" in the sense that they regard the office of county commissioner as tied to politics. The clerk fills the anomalous position of being essential to the functions of the local government process but holding the least understood of county positions.

The authors have conducted this study with the purpose of recording the role of clerks in Florida's history and placing the office in its historical and contemporary context. No effort has been made to be comprehensive because that would require years to accomplish. Still, the authors have examined pertinent state and local documents, newspapers, diaries, contemporary letters, and secondary articles and books relating to the subject, and they also have interviewed a number of clerks and other knowledgeable people. The contributions of the people we talked with are acknowledged in the text and in the bibliography. We wish to give special thanks to Roger Alderman; Barbara Nettles, Director Member Services; and Laurie A. LoRe', senior government analyst for the Association. By no means the final word, this study, the authors hope, will be a useful introduction.

William Warren Rogers
Canter Brown, Jr.

ACKNOWLEDGMENTS

The authors gratefully appreciate the kind assistance and helpful contributions of a number of individuals and institutions in the preparation of this history. Particularly important were Leland Hawes, *Tampa Tribune*; Tom Muir, Historic Pensacola Preservation Board; Nathan Woolsey, Milton; David J. Coles, Florida State Archives; and James M. Denham, Florida Southern College, Lakeland. We also thank the staffs of the Florida Association of Court Clerks and Comptrollers and of the Florida Collection of the State Library of Florida.

Chapter 1

Beginnings

As will be explored in the pages that follow, for almost two hundred years clerks of Florida's county and circuit courts have provided services to the people so essential that it is difficult to imagine the fair, efficient, or responsive administration of government without their contributions. Indeed, it could be said that the county clerk stands as the most-unique local official in the state's history. Since the clerks and their staffs usually have worked quietly and without notoriety, their achievements often have gone unrecognized. Notwithstanding that fact, they have withstood challenges of frontier life, political conflict, Indian war, Civil War, Reconstruction, constitutional and statutory revisions, boom and bust economies, staggering increases in workload due to dramatic population growth, and demands of technological innovation coupled with increasingly severe budgetary constraints.

Before relating the details of the clerks' story, though, a few words might be in order to provide necessary context. While a prolonged discussion of the evolution of our governmental and legal concepts would not be appropriate here, two themes pertinent to the clerks' historical role should be sounded. First, when the law is mentioned, what is meant? Second, how have Americans come to organize their government to achieve justice through law?

That a circuit clerk must deal with the law seems plain, as does the fact that no courts would exist in the absence of laws. From early in history the interactions of human beings necessitated the evolution of rules of conduct. Custom dictated the first laws, and, as the rules became more complicated and numerous, formal governments were born. With them came the need for written laws. The Hammurabic Code of 2350 B.C. constitutes the earliest-known system of such written laws and has brought renown to its author Hammurabi, the king of the Amorites who controlled Mesopotamia, the cradle of civilization in the Middle East.

Two systems, civil law and common law, have most influenced present-day western civilization. Civil law derived from enactments of the Roman senate and, thus, is statutory in nature. It remains of central importance in much of Europe, particularly because of the influence of France's Napoleonic Code. Louisiana in the United States traces its legal system to the French model. Elsewhere in the United States, the law and legal systems owe much of their origins to English common law, which evolved from Anglo-Saxon foundations. The diverse experiences of the British Isles over a millennium molded and adapted the common law. When the British crown began issuing charters for American colonies in the seventeenth century, as a matter of course the common law and the character of legal institutions associated with it translated themselves, at least in spirit, to the New World.

From the days of the Hammurabic Code, if not before, the administration of law posed problems. If skilled individuals were required to craft and administer the rules of conduct, then experts also were needed to interpret them. The ancient Greeks, for example, realized the need for a distinct set of men, judges, to pass on the intent and meaning of the government's strictures. Gradually, special officers trained in the law applied themselves to the task, but, often, they also performed other duties for the government that were nonjudicial in nature.

To modern eyes, the mixture of judicial and nonjudicial responsibilities in a government officer might appear as a conflict of interest undermining the judiciary's integrity and independence. Yet, such perspectives took a long time in finding widespread adoption. Numerous English philosophers and legal scholars of the seventeenth and eighteenth century speculated on the nature of justice and the most-desirable organization for its fair administration, but the French philosophe Montesquieu struck one of the stronger chords. His famous *The Spirit of the Laws*, published in 1748, insisted that the creation of a just form of government required separation of executive, legislative, and judicial powers. Such a system of checks and balances would protect and guarantee freedom. His thesis gained implementation when written into the United States Constitution in 1787, having already been adopted by several of the new state constitutions.

Thus, a separate judicial system long has been an accepted and necessary part of American democracy. Key to the success of an independent judiciary, though, has been the need for an independent officer to tend to the nuts and bolts of its everyday administration, to ensure the integrity of its procedures, and to protect the documentary evidence essential to its deliberations and the lives and fortunes of local residents. As will be seen, Floridians grasped this need from the first days after the Spanish colony became an American possession, but they saw still more. While many other southern states and territories entrusted the administration of county affairs to other officers, Floridians entrusted the responsibilities to their court clerks.

Chapter

2

The Territorial Years
(1821 - 1845)

It began with Andrew Jackson during the summer of 1821. During the previous decade the American general twice had invaded Spanish Florida. The second occasion, known as the First Seminole War, prompted the king of Spain and his government to enter negotiations for the colony's transfer to the United States under the best terms available. The resulting Adams-Onis Treaty of 1819 finally achieved ratification by the United States Senate in January 1821. At first President James Monroe had thought to send Jackson, a national hero since his victory over the British at New Orleans six years earlier, to Russia rather than back to Florida. The plans changed when Thomas Jefferson convinced the President that the volatile general would spark a quarrel with the Czar within a month. Accordingly, Monroe dispatched Jackson south.

Additional causes exacerbated Jackson's irritability that year, a situation that would affect his tenure as governor and influence his perception of the role of clerk of courts. He insisted to others that he desired an end to the rigors of public life, and a chronic cough combined with lung problems to undermine his health. Word of his reputation for impatience with diplomacy circulated widely, and he chafed at presidential restrictions on his ability to pursue some of his most-bitter enemies, Red Stick Creek Indians from Alabama and their free black allies who had taken refuge from Jackson in the Florida peninsula. The general's close associates also knew that Mrs. Rachel Jackson dreaded the trials of life in remote Florida. Doubtlessly, she concurred with sentiments expressed by Virginian John Randolph. "Florida, sir, is not worth buying," the congressman declared. "It is a land of swamps, of quagmires, of frogs and alligators and mosquitoes!" He concluded: "No, sir! No man would immigrate to Florida-- no, not from hell itself!"[1]

Jackson accepted the transfer of possession at Pensacola on July 17. Technically his act related only to West Florida, the former English and Spanish colony that lay between the Perdido and Suwannee rivers. East Florida, centered on its capital at St. Augustine, had accepted American control one week earlier. Nonetheless, Jackson's authority ran throughout the vast and sparsely populated possession, and he acted with dispatch to organize its government. As his men raised the American flag, he pledged that "all laws and municipal regulations which were in existence at the cessation of the late government, remain in full force."[2] Then, in a series of proclamations issued over the next several weeks, he remade the face of government.

One of the provisional governor's first acts resulted in the creation of two counties, Escambia out of West Florida and St. Johns in the east, to provide local governmental services other than those offered town residents by Pensacola and St. Augustine. For both counties he authorized a court composed of justices of the peace. Not later than July 19 Jackson exerted his authority to control appointment of the court's clerk, and he did so before he named the presiding judge. His designee was John Miller. Pursuant to Jackson's direction, the acting governor in East Florida similarly filled key positions in St. Johns County. There a former Englishman, George Gibbs, received the nod as county clerk.

John Miller's appointment as Florida's first court clerk in the American era spoke volumes about Jackson's view of the clerk's powers and responsibilities. In Miller, he had chosen a trusted military aide, one who held the rank of lieutenant colonel and had long been associated with the governor. Enjoying strong connections with Kentucky's political establishment, Miller would receive enthusiastic support for his career from United States Senator John J. Crittenden, Governor William T. Barry, and prominent leader J. C. Breckinridge. A Pensacola newspaper would laud his "zeal and ability," while Jackson considered him "a man of sterling worth--and under all circumstances to be relied on."[3] Before 1821 had ended, Miller would assume additional duties as Pensacola's mayor and later would sit on the territory's legislative council.

Jackson needed to be able to rely upon his clerk. The governor's personal situation--including his problems with health, frustration, fatigue, and irritability--propelled him to execute his responsibilities expeditiously. The duties were numerous, and many of them required the clerk's participation and assistance. For one thing, the transfer of possession from Spain involved complicated claims, differing legal systems, and dissimilar languages, not to mention conflicts of personality and uncertainty of applicable law and procedure. Perhaps as importantly, the governor needed someone who would seek aggressively to obtain and maintain pertinent land records and related legal documents. Many of Jackson's friends and protégés, including future territorial political giants such as Richard Keith Call and James Gadsden, had come to Florida in the hopes of building their fortunes from land speculation and plantation development. Their aspirations depended upon clarification of land titles and control of the records.

In the situation the governor hesitated little before dispatching Miller upon these duties. Particularly, he directed the clerk and two other representatives to examine documents remaining in the custody of holdover

Spanish officials and to demand those deemed necessary or helpful for resolution of ongoing legal disputes. The attempt to carry out Jackson's directive brought Miller and his associates into conflict with the Spanish officialdom. The ensuing confrontation placed the clerk and the governor in the center of an international furor when the governor ordered the arrest of the former Spanish governor of West Florida.

If nothing else, the incident of the Spanish governor's arrest illustrated the central role Jackson planned for his clerk of choice to play, and that role extended beyond judicial responsibilities to an executive role in local affairs. As mentioned, the governor erected as each county's governing authority a court of five justices of the peace, with powers similar to those later bestowed upon boards of county commissioners. A quorum of the justices could set policy that, presumably, the clerk would then administer. Details of the workings of the arrangement are elusive, but a precedent had been set that would shortly be followed when Florida's government received a more-formal organization.

The insight Jackson displayed in recognizing the importance of the county clerk mirrored his concerns as to filling other Florida clerkships. President Monroe had designated men to preside in federal courts in East and West Florida, but had left vague their powers and jurisdiction. The governor stepped into the vacuum by asserting his right to name the district court clerks. While the situation remains murky, seemingly Jackson intended the West Florida position for John Miller. The court barely had begun to organize, though, when the judge departed the territory after a confrontation with Jackson. In East Florida a Virginian, James S. Tingle, assumed the post pursuant to Jackson's authority. When the judge--one-time Kentucky Congressman William Pope DuVal--arrived in November, he reacted angrily to the presumption. "Under a belief that such an act would not be either legal or proper," he informed Secretary of State John Quincy Adams, "I feel it my duty to reject any that may be so appointed and shall appoint a Clerk myself [unless directed otherwise]."[4] For the moment, Jackson prevailed.

At the time of DuVal's attack on Jackson's authority, the careers of both men and Florida history already had begun to change. Never pleased with his Florida responsibilities and home, the governor departed for Tennessee in October and resigned his position in early November. "I can only observe for the present that I am truly wearied of public life," he informed President Monroe. "I want to rest."[5] DuVal hurried himself to Washington to secure the vacancy.

William Pope DuVal's quest succeeded in 1822, and, properly speaking, he became Florida's first territorial governor since his appointment came after enactment by the Congress of a statute formally organizing the Territory of Florida. That 1822 law created federal superior courts for districts of East and West Florida that would operate on the county level as the basic trial court. Eventually, the Congress added three more districts as population growth and business development demanded. As specified in the act, each judge could designate a clerk, thereby resolving the DuVal-Jackson feud of the previous year.

The territorial act contained other provisions of significance to Florida. As to the judiciary, it specified that the governor and a presidentially appointed (later elective) legislative council could supplement the federal system with lower courts. The council soon acted in that regard, and in doing so followed Andrew Jackson's earlier model. The county court now consisted of three judges appointed by the governor, but the statute supplemented its limited judicial authority with the powers of a county commission. The law additionally provided, in part, "That there shall be appointed in each county a well qualified clerk, whose duty it shall be to record all decrees, orders, judgments, and other papers required by law, and to preserve all papers appertaining to suits in said courts, and who shall take an oath faithfully to perform the duties, which have or may hereafter be assigned to him." The officer's term ran for two years, unless earlier removed by the governor and council. He could take office only after posting an approved $2,000 performance bond. Once again, the clerk served as the court's executive arm.[6]

Through the territorial period clerks of both superior and county courts endured a myriad of hardships and challenges. As local courts proliferated when the council carved out new counties such as Jackson, Gadsden, Leon, Columbia, Duval, and Monroe, clerks faced problems stemming from the very unpopularity of the tribunal. "Of all the institutions of territorial government," observed historian James M. Denham, "county courts were probably the most criticized." He continued, "Local citizens often complained that its tax assessing powers were unfair and its decisions were arbitrary."[7] A St. Augustine editor in 1830 put the issue more squarely, accusing local judges of a willingness to purchase influence with "corrupt patronage."[8]

In many new counties clerks dealt with frontier conditions that multiplied the efforts required to perform faithfully their assigned tasks. As late as the 1840s Hillsborough County's clerk E. A. Ware summed up the dilemma in a plea to higher officials:

> *When I took office, there were neither books, forms nor any thing else! Two books are used--one for all the dockets and the other for the minutes of court. I want several other books, but am unable to learn the proper person to apply to for them. I had to rent an office and furnish it entirely with desks, tables, etc. which I understood the law makes no provision for and I never have received any laws until recently, and being entirely unacquainted with the routine of such matters--errors in form are unavoidable at the outset. I made out my a/c under the instruction of the judge and solicitor, and if you think it necessary to audit it you must do it--though as the duties were performed therein charged I should think it rather hard upon an officer, whose office is by no means a sinecure one. . . . There was [sic] no law books nor advice to be queried by which will in measure account for the looseness manifested in making out the accounts.*[9]

Clerk Ware's complaints echoed, sometimes more loudly, in the territorial experiences of many of his peers. As will be discussed more fully in a subsequent chapter, often after a county's creation local residents pressed into service as a courthouse the private home of the clerk or some other individual until a proper structure could be erected. Even then, the most simple of buildings sometimes had to suffice. In Hillsborough County's case, citizens put together a log cabin, reportedly costing a mere $200. Underscoring the frontier nature of much of Florida life, the Spartan courthouse quickly suffered destruction during an Indian attack at the onset of the Second Seminole War.

The availability of adequate facilities and supplies aside, clerks often fought simply to get paid for their work. Governor Jackson had established a fee schedule during the early days of the American era. He directed that a clerk would receive: for every citation, $1.00; for entering an order, 50 cents; for administering and writing oaths, 12 cents; for filing petitions, interrogatories, and answers, & c. 20 cents; for entering judgment, $1.00; for executions, $1.00; for summons to witnesses, 50 cents; for making copies, 25 cents per 100 words; and, for taking depositions, 25 cents. Jackson further permitted "compensation as the court for which he is appointed may from time to time, and in each suit, tax or allow."[10] In 1824 the legislative council followed with a general law prescribing a similar system.

Although compensation was provided for, the kinds of problems encountered by Hillsborough's E. A. Ware in obtaining remuneration confronted other clerks, including those appointed for the federal trial courts. By 1824, Pensacola's John Miller served as clerk of the West Florida superior court. In September his deputy informed the United States

Secretary of State that the "court commenced operations here in October 1822." He continued, "The Clerk's accounts have regularly been made out, certified by the Judge & forwarded to the proper department at Washington by the Marshal; owing to the accounts for Territorial business being included they were not allowed, but information was received that they would be returned here to take out the charges exclusively on United States' business which would then be paid; this was more than three months ago & <u>the accounts have not been received back yet</u>. There is upwards of $700 due the Clerk on U.S. business only, which he is thus deprived of, either by accident or neglect."[11]

Four years afterward Deputy Clerk William H. Hunt, now clerk in his own right, found himself required to petition the Congress about another compensation problem. "Your Petitioner most respectfully represents," Hunt declared, "that he has never been allowed or received one dollar as a per diem allowance or compensation for attending the United States' District & Superior Court of West Florida as Clerk thereof--but that his accounts therefore, though regularly examined allowed and signed by the Hon the Judge of said Court, have uniformly been disallowed & rejected."[12] The frustration felt when the Congress declined to act on the complaint doubtlessly was shared by many other clerks.

Yet another challenge arose for clerks because of confusion as to just how they were to be selected. With respect to their jurisdiction, county courts held an intermediate position between justices of the peace and superior courts. Additionally, the officers of the county courts accepted responsibilities similar to those of modern county commissioners. The county clerks' relationship with the courts approximated, though under less-well-defined circumstances, that of the modern era. Similarly, clerks of the superior courts were integrally bound to their respective tribunals which, after statehood in 1845, became the modern circuit courts.

Confusion proliferated in territorial Florida from the fact that the same person usually performed the role of county clerk and superior court clerk and, further, because the law failed to specify clearly just how each was to get his job. Separate laws applied to both varieties of clerks, and the results produced ambiguities and inconsistencies. A legislative council enactment of 1822, for example, provided for clerks in Duval and St. Johns counties who would serve as records keepers and who would be appointed by the territorial governor.[13] The legislation failed to specify how long the clerks would serve, the presumption being that tenure was based on "good behavior." The next year, when the territorial assembly created three more counties, a new law vested authority for appointing county clerks in the governor and the legislative council.[14] A separate measure specified that the governor and council possessed appointive authority for county clerks of Duval County.[15] Even so, in 1824 an act pertaining the superior courts for the Eastern District empowered the judge to appoint the clerk.[16]

For several years after this flurry of legislation, few initiatives of significance affected the clerks and their confusing situation. Then, in

November 1828 the council passed a law that required a clerk in each county court but failed to say who would appoint him. Yet, the act's provisions contained more specificity than some of the earlier ones: the clerk was to hold office for two years and be subject to removal by the governor.[17] One month afterward another statute enabled judges to designate superior court clerks and required the already traditional $2,000 bond, while charging incumbents with the "faithful performance of duty."[18]

To these measures, solons appended a third 1828 enactment broadly revising the territory's judicial system, as a part of which duties of court clerks were enumerated. A catch-all clause required all county clerks (also sheriffs, coroners, surveyors, assessors, and collectors of taxes) to be popularly elected on a "general ticket."[19] Apparently the United States Congress objected to this implementation of Jacksonian democracy, for the council the following year mandated the appointment of all county clerks (without saying by whom) and permitted them to serve two years as long as they behaved themselves.[20] Adding complexity to confusion, in 1833 legislators again revisited the clerks, now insisting that they be "commissioned" by unnamed officials.[21]

During the remaining twelve turbulent years of Florida's territorial period, county and circuit court clerks remained on the job despite the muddled state of affairs. Two examples provide illustrations of interesting occurrences growing out of their situation. First, in 1832 Dennis Hankins ran for county clerk in Madison County. Although it was a popular election, the resourceful Hankins had seen to it that the voting place was his home, and, as the only candidate, he enjoyed election by a unanimous vote.[22] On the other hand, an act of 1844 finally organized a superior court for Mosquito County, which had been created two decades earlier (not until 1845 would the county receive its modern name of Orange). Among other things, that law specifically empowered the judge to appoint a clerk, who could barely have entered upon his duties before the coming of statehood in 1845 changed everything once again.[23]

It is clear now, though it was hardly so at the time, that, despite demands made in the name of Jacksonian democracy to let the people decide who should be their county and superior court clerks, this often was not the case in territorial Florida. Yet, if many clerks were appointed by the judges, there were numerous exceptions. Jacksonian democracy would finally prevail, but it resulted only after a bitter political fight that helped give birth to Florida's political parties.

Chapter 3

The Constitution of 1838 - 1939, Statehood, and the Clerks

The desire of most Floridians to exercise the right of electing public officials--a yearning paralleled through the nation during the late 1820s and 1830s and known, after President Andrew Jackson, as the era of Jacksonian democracy--finally found at least partial satisfaction when Florida became a state in 1845. On the other hand, the constitution which specified those rights had been drafted over six years earlier amid political turmoil and in the face of arguments for splitting Florida into two parts. Political wounds had opened that would not heal before the nation, itself, split into warring parts in 1861. And, in that political struggle the office of clerk of courts played a controversial role.

Since the first years of the territorial period, most residents had assumed that statehood would be for Florida the next logical step. By the mid-1830s, though, a series of events had shaken the cooperative alliance between East Floridians and the ever-growing and evermore-influential Middle Florida section between the Apalachicola and Suwannee rivers. In the latter region large cotton plantations worked by black slaves produced wealth to support an affluent planter society centered at Tallahassee and in smaller towns such as Marianna, Quincy, Monticello, and Madison. East Florida developed quite differently. There subsistence farming, cattle grazing, lumbering, and marine stores industries underlay a society in which the plantation system made fewer inroads, where northern-born residents exerted greater influence, and where race relations patterns maintained some flexibility reminiscent of Spanish colonial days.

Then, in 1835 came an event disastrous for the territory that, in turn, set in motion the steps leading toward a constitutional convention and eventual statehood. In December of that year Indians and free blacks in the peninsula revolted against efforts of the Jackson administration to force them to immigrate from Florida to a western reservation. Hundreds of slaves at farms and plantations surrounding Indian lands also revolted, prompting what was, arguably, the largest slave revolt in United States history. When they did so, a territorial council dominated by Middle Florida planters passed a law that penalized East Florida planters whose slaves had gone to war, an action that resulted in tremendous rancor in East Florida aimed at Middle Florida planters.[24]

Other events then complicated matters further. As East Floridians "forted up" in isolated frontier locations and the hostiles exerted control over most of the peninsula, the nation entered into an economic depression known as the Panic of 1837. The combination of circumstances shook Florida's financial institutions, particularly Middle Florida's Union Bank. When that bank and its sister institutions began to call loans and deposits seemed jeopardized, East Floridians' attitudes hardened against the Middle Florida planters. In the situation the planters determined to grab control of affairs to prevent the East from going its own way and to forestall collapse of the territorial banks in which they were so heavily invested.

As leader of the Middle Florida planter society, Governor Richard Keith Call initiated action in 1837 by calling for a territory-wide vote on statehood. With many East Florida men serving in volunteer companies, the tally came in at 2,214 in favor and 1,274 opposed, with the East overwhelmingly opposed. The next year Call urged the council to call a convention to draft a suitable constitution. With war yet raging in the peninsula, voters selected delegates in October. They convened at the Gulf coast boom town of St. Joseph on December 3.[25]

The St. Joseph convention saw East and Middle Floridians, pro-bank and anti-bank forces, and pro-statehood and anti-statehood men battle over the territory's future. The gathering contained many of Florida's most-prominent leaders. One of the few East Florida pro-statehood men, Robert Raymond Reid, a native of South Carolina and United States judge, achieved election as convention president with the votes of Middle Floridians. He defeated former governor William Pope DuVal, then of Calhoun County in West Florida. Pursuant to the powers granted him, Reid appointed various committees and their chairmen, so that specialized groups could draft specific portions of the constitution. That process consumed almost six weeks, marked mostly by hot debate and hotter feelings. In the end, on January 11, 1839, a document found approval of all but one of the fifty-six men present.[26]

The convention's deliberations dealt directly with the question of clerks of court. As has been seen, confusion existed as to how county and superior court clerks secured office, and the delegates moved to correct the ambiguity. The clerks' fate lay especially with chairman Richard C. Allen of Calhoun County, soon to become a superior court judge himself, and the Committee on the Judicial Department. Its members included United States Senator-to-be James D. Westcott, Jr., of Leon; future supreme court justice Thomas Baltzell of Jackson; George T. Ward of Leon; and James M. Partridge of Calhoun. Necessarily the provisions of the Judicial article (Article V) affected the clerks, and so they were addressed ultimately in that article's section 13. Overall the final constitution would provide for a state supreme court, as well as courts of chancery (never established), circuit

courts (there would be four judicial circuits which were the equivalent of the territorial superior courts), and justices of the peace. The territorial county court would be dropped. The general assembly was directed to establish by law a probate court in each county. As for the clerks of the new circuit courts, they were to be chosen by popular election, even though most state officers and the circuit judges would be selected by the legislature.[27]

Popular election for clerks found a place in the constitution, but not without a fight that began with the judiciary committee's report. That document, submitted December 10, provided: "The clerk of the superior [intended to be supreme] court, and the clerks of the circuit courts, in this State, shall be appointed by the Judges thereof, and to hold the office at the will of the court."[28] Given the domination of the judiciary committee and the convention by high-powered lawyers, merchants, and planter politicians, such a recommendation should not have come as a surprise. As historian Dorothy Dodd concluded of the assembly as a whole, "In its provisions for the selection of officers, the convention evidenced a distrust both of the people and of the executive."[29]

With that background, the proposal for appointive clerks settled on the convention. On December 20 debate first focused on the judicial article as the assembly met as a committee of the whole. Interestingly, the convention's proceedings noted only that "After some time spent in its consideration, the committee arose, reported progress, and asked leave to sit again, which was concurred in."[30] Apparently, the general language masked the fact that the delegates had sensed enough pressure from their constituents to replace immediately the provision for appointive clerks with a mandate for popular election. If so, the action certainly signifies the special nature of the office in the eyes of Florida voters. The section, as adjusted by the convention, read:

> *"The Clerk of the Supreme Court, and the Clerks of the Courts of Chancery, shall be elected by the General Assembly; and the Clerks of the Circuit Courts, shall be elected by the qualified electors, in such mode as may be prescribed by law."*[31]

The clash of ideology had not ended. On December 21, 1838, Article V, as adjusted, was ordered engrossed for its third and final reading. Christmas day then witnessed further consideration of the judicial provisions. Former governor DuVal quickly launched an assault aimed at placing appointment and tenure of clerks in the hands of judges. Every member of the judicial article committee save for Westcott voted with him, but the attempt failed by a vote of 24 to 31. The clash proved to be the final one respecting organization of Florida's first state judiciary. As the convention proceedings thereupon noted, "The article on the Judicial Department was then on motion adopted."[32]

Next came the battle over popular ratification. After a hotly contested campaign conducted against the background of a continuing Second Seminole War, the election was held May 6, 1839. The vote was close, with the clerks playing an important--though still unclear--role in the process, politically and in the tallying and transmission of elections results. Using wartime disruptions as an excuse, Governor Call failed to report the vote totals until August. The figures he released were 2,071 in favor of ratification, while those opposed to statehood numbered 1,958, a margin of 113 votes. East Florida again overwhelmingly defeated the initiative.[33]

The matter did not end there. The poorly written article of the constitution that called for the election failed to state which official, the governor or the convention president, would announce the final vote or even receive the tallies. As president, Robert Raymond Reid appealed to county court clerks to send him certified copies of the results, convinced that Call's totals were incomplete and likely incorrect. At first, Reid declined to release the information gained thereby. Instead, on October 21 he proclaimed ratification without a mention of the majority by which it was gained. Later, when he served as territorial governor, Reid insisted that 2,070 favored the constitution and 1,975 opposed it.[34]

For over half a decade Floridians continued their struggle over statehood. The convention's debates sparked the creation of two political parties, a split that mirrored national political developments at the time. Democrats favored the national administration of Andrew Jackson's successor Martin Van Buren, statehood, state's rights, and limitations on banks. Whigs in Middle Florida urged statehood and banking, while East Florida Whigs fought like tigers to divorce their section from Middle Florida domination. In the end a pro-statehood East Florida Democrat, David Levy

[Yulee], made the difference. As congressional delegate, he convinced national lawmakers to admit Florida to the Union in 1845 as a slave state to balance the admission of free-state Iowa. John Tyler inked the law on March 3, 1845, his last full day as President, adding in Florida's honor a twenty-seventh star to the United States flag.[35]

Chapter

4

Courthouses, Trials, Tribulations, and Personalities

It goes without saying that, before clerks and other officials can perform their various duties, they need to be properly housed. Under normal conditions territorial-era county clerks, clerks of the superior court, and, after statehood in 1845, circuit clerks had their offices in courthouses or in smaller, adjacent buildings. Yet, Florida contained during most of the nineteenth century one of the United States' last frontiers.[36] In the circumstances clerks often had to make do with what was available. Courthouses, stores, and offices in frontier Florida towns generally were log structures, but building even a log courthouse took time and effort.

Meanwhile, demands upon county government persisted. The problems remained through the century.

The 1887 formation of Citrus County provides an illustration. Its initial seat of government was Mannfield. The county commissioners convened first in the Mannfield church, while the Moffat house became the temporary courthouse, where W. C. Zimmerman served as the first circuit clerk. In 1892, the commissioners were compelled to rent the Gaffney house as a second courthouse, for the princely sum of $19 per month. That year county residents, after fierce struggles, finally voted to move the county seat to Inverness, a trading post town incorporated only in 1883 and itself retaining a distinct frontier flavor.[37]

The rough and often transitory nature of county facilities also can be seen in the experience of Madison County. Legislators carved that entity out of Jefferson County in 1827, with Hixtown (Hickstown) designated as a site for county government. At a subsequent point San Pedro emerged as the first official county seat. Madison's first county court met there in the home of Mrs. Elizabeth Carter, a widow. Local residents in 1832 erected as a courthouse a log structure with one room and a fireplace at one end. The county seat thereafter was moved to Newton, the name of which was changed in 1838 to Madison. Its first framed courthouse achieved completion in 1840.[38] Marion County shared a similar experience in the humble origins of its public facilities. Created in March 1844 while Florida remained a territory, Marion (with Fort King as its seat) became the twenty-fourth county. Alexander McLeod, a Georgian, received a commission as the first clerk of court in October of that year. Each morning he left his residence in one of the buildings on the post and reported to work at the courthouse. That structure consisted of a two-story, cupola-topped barracks for the enlisted men. With statehood yet pending, McLeod filed his first instrument of record, which consisted of a mortgage foreclosure against a colonel of the post.

Progress came to Marion county by leaps and bounds in 1846, as old names and old facilities were left behind. Fort King saw itself transformed into the frontier village of Ocala, and a small log building replaced the barracks as courthouse. The new county building enjoyed the advantage of having a spring and large trees nearby. Its appearance reflected a square, one-story structure whose walls were composed of peeled pine trees. Three sides had a door and a window. The sturdy edifice, with its wood doors and shutters (all hung by massive handwrought iron hinges), cost $225, with an extra $80 for a judge's bench, jury box, and interior furnishings. Fortunately, the courthouse was not too austere to prevent the Masonic lodge from holding its meetings there.[39]

Jefferson County's courthouse saga reflected a more-ambitious scheme, one expected of an affluent Middle Florida plantation county. The first building, not surprisingly for 1827, was John Robinson's log house. Finally local men erected a wooden courthouse in 1841. It was two-storied, measured fifty feet square, and proudly boasted a bell that the night watchman rang to mark the hours of darkness. The early days often saw empty court dockets, but the clerk still had plenty to do, not the least of which was his responsibility for performing marriages. During the 1820s and 1830s the zealous clerk even attempted to ensure the permanence of his ceremonies by requiring a prospective husband to sign a $2,000 bond that he would fulfill the conditions of the marriage contract.[40]

Grander days awaited Jefferson County in 1848, when a new courthouse, costing $3,897, opened for business. As was the case with its counterparts in many other counties, the facility became a community center for political rallies, church services, and theatrical productions. Chess and checkers players, as well as idlers who dispensed free advice and wisdom, gathered there. The availability of the facility was so prized that, not until 1915, was the sheriff permitted to regulate the entertainments offered there.[41]

On the other end of the scale, remote counties such as old Manatee made do until well into the century with facilities of a most-primitive nature. In 1876 court clerk John Francis Bartholf described his experience in creating a county site at Pine Level, located on the prairie between the modern cities of Bradenton and Arcadia:

> *During the winter of 1865 & 1866--the State Legislature passed an Act entitled an Act to locate the County Seat of Manatee County[,] in accordance with the provisions of which a Board of Commissioners selected this locality, and conferred on it the name as above stated--to be the County Seat of Manatee County--*

> *Immediate steps were taken by the Board of County Commissioners to erect a Court House, and there being no saw mills in the County, a rough log house 20 x 30--clapboard roof & puncheon floor--with seats of similar material were constructed in which to hold the Courts of the County--and such has remained the accommodation for the transaction of such business until this year when steps are being taken to erect a suitable frame building. Whether they will be effected or not in the face of the opposition manifested at home and abroad, time alone can tell--*
>
> *Pine Level, remained[--]as found[--]a barren unsettled wilderness, with nought to distinguish it from the surrounding country save the rude Court House referred to, its nearest settler a mile distant for several years. In 1869 the author of this sketch--Clerk of the Circuit Court--a native of New York City-- and Captain in the U.S. Army during the war, in the face of considerable prejudice and some opposition, raising mainly from an old fogy idea then very prevalent (and not dead yet) with some people that the county belonged to them though not owning a foot of land--settled near the Court House and hewed from the stump a rude log house--and the necessary fencing material to enclose a few acres of land. Thus Pine Level got its first settler. Up to the present time its population has only been increased by four families--three white & one colored--with another in prospective. There has been but little improvement in the style of its buildings[,] they being mostly both public & private[,] being constructed of logs--including in the number two store houses--jail & Jury house.[42]*

Testifying to the veracity of Bartholf's comments about Pine Level and the rough circumstances under which he labored is the account of a visitor there on court day in January 1870:

> *We paid a flying visit to Pine Level, Manatee county, last week, and had an opportunity of seeing what the people down that way were doing, &c. . . . Monday was County Court day, and a good many of the Manateeites were out there, all prepared with three feeds of corn for their horses, and wallets well filled with "hities" [Hayti potatoes], beef, pork, biscuit, rice, sausages, and sugar and coffee for themselves and interloping friends. Besides these good things every man had*

his blanket and at night all gathered around large lightwood fires, wrapped themselves in their blankets, and slept as comfortably as if they had been in a first class hotel. Judge [Enoch E.] Mizell promptly dispatched the business in Court and then all hands homeward bent their way.[43]

That circuit clerks performed unorthodox services and courthouses served uses other than for county government, as was shown a few paragraphs ago in the case of Jefferson County, offers an ongoing statement about the frontier and democracy. Examples proliferated in Florida of the multiple uses of the principal county building, two of which point out the varied situations with which clerks were compelled to deal in the daily course of their affairs. First, the courthouse in Manatee County was commandeered during one period for a school, although the donation was not entirely philanthropic. Officials compelled the academy's patrons to agree to pay for all damages to the property.[44] Then, just a few miles to the north and east at Polk County's seat of Bartow, the two-story courthouse on the square, erected in 1867 from the generosity of cattleman Jacob Summerlin, briefly served to unite God and mammon when it was used for a church. In such circumstances, the distractions must have proved an onerous burden to any purposeful clerk.[45]

Forced to deal with a myriad of challenges as part of their normal responsibilities, clerks nonetheless often found local officials unresponsive to their demands for essential supplies and equipment. In that regard the Clay County clerk experienced great fortune, though it took until 1911, when the board of county commissioners, responding to repeated pleas, at last declared the clerk's facilities "entirely inadequate, both in the office and vaults, for safe keeping of records." As a result, the handsome amount of $8,000 was decreed for an addition to the courthouse at Green Cove Springs to upgrade his office and records and secure a reliable vault.[46]

Once a courthouse and appropriate facilities were built or otherwise made available, keeping them involved quite another problem. Many Florida courthouses suffered damage by fire. The causes ranged from accidental to deliberate, and they often resulted in complete or, at least, extensive destruction. Columbia County endured probably more repeated tragedies of this sort than any other. The train of fiery events commenced after Columbia, created in 1832, moved beyond its private-residence courthouse stage. Then, residents of the county seat of Alligator (renamed Lake City in 1859) witnessed the burning of its courthouse on four occasions--in 1846, 1860, 1867, and 1874. The 1846 conflagration struck both the county building and the nearby store of G. D. Miller. Even as the flames rose, a lawyer stabbed Miller with a jack knife because he believed his victim had accused him of setting the fire. Miller recovered, and Alligator's citizens reached common agreement that both fires were an incendiary's work, although no one was arrested. Officials blamed the 1874 fire on the existing Reconstruction-era political situation, but rumors persisted that some indicted hog thieves supposedly torched the building to destroy evidence against them.[47]

Most courthouse fires involved suspicious circumstances, but few culprits endured arrest or conviction. The Jackson County facility burned in December 1848, destroying all county records along with the building. According to the Marianna *Florida Whig*, the origin of the 3:00 A. M. fire was "unknown--it is supposed to have been the work of an incendiary." The journal continued, "The night, fortunately, was calm, and by vigilance, the fire was prevented from communicating to the surrounding buildings."[48] A few months afterward the Gadsden County courthouse at Quincy flared, also between three and four in the morning. The building and its records, except for the trial docket of the current term, were lost. "No doubt is entertained," one newspaper reported, "but that it was the villainous work of an incendiary."[49] Ominously, after Columbia County's 1860 tragedy, a local man confided to his diary, "The Citizens are holding a meeting tonight to organize a vigilance committee."[50]

Even from the distance of the present, clerks of some counties whose courthouses burned command sympathy, if only because the process of locating and constructing the facilities proved so tortuous and the circumstances of their destruction so bizarre. A case in point arises out of Orange County. Mosquito County, as Orange was known prior to 1845, first boasted county seats at New Smyrna and also at Enterprise (Benson Springs). Fort Gatlin, the future Orlando, came into existence in 1838, initially as a military post and then as the homestead of the Aaron Jernigan family. In 1856 lawmakers divided the county, with Volusia going its own way, and

Jernigan (renamed the next year as Orlando) became the new county seat of Orange. Alabamian B. F. Caldwell donated four acres of land for a courthouse, but it was not built due to lack of necessary funds. Clerk James Hughey and other officials found themselves ensconced in spartan surroundings: an old, deserted two-room log house that had no windows and only a dirt floor.

The situation began to improve for the clerk in 1863, when a courthouse was erected on Caldwell's four acres, amid proper Confederate ceremonies. Still, the building could not have been called ostentatious. It possessed one door and two rooms, one down and one up. It lasted five years. Then, in 1868 a case involving cattle rustlers and related evidence found its way before the bar of local justice, and, before anyone realized what was happening, the courthouse went up in flames. Later, investigators uncovered bottles of turpentine and inflammable resin along one side of the gutted structure. The poor county officials, faced with the loss of most of their records, rented a house for $10 per month to serve as office space. One small victory permitted both the clerk and the sheriff a set of keys. In 1875, thanks to a $10,000 loan from cattleman Jacob Summerlin, a replacement courthouse eventually arose from the ashes, doubtlessly to the delight of the incumbent officeholders.[51]

As is quite evident in Orange County's case and in others mentioned in this chapter, the process of moving county seats added greatly to the demands placed upon the clerk. Florida formed new counties as demographics or politics demanded, but legislators also relocated county seats in a seemingly never-ending stream of actions. Naturally, the selection or removal of a county seat stirred considerable local controversy, particularly in the town or towns that lost. To give up the status and the money that went with being the seat of government sometimes delivered a killer blow to a community and always carried a negative impact. Of course, the clerk, in such instances, found himself taxed with the costs of uprooting his family, perhaps selling his business and other properties, and making a new home in a community quite possibly hostile to him.

The experience of Alachua County shows what a community and its citizens might suffer or gain. Formed in 1824, Alachua County saw its first county courthouse constructed at Newnansville (originally known as Dell's). In 1832, with the creation of Columbia County, Newnansville was included in the new subdivision. County court for Alachua then met in private homes, and in 1836 at Spring Grove. When the legislative council restored Newnansville to Alachua and re-established it as the county seat in 1839, the old courthouse still stood. Although previously deserted by the county court, it had served to accommodate the superior court for Alachua and Columbia. Given the building's small size, on some occasions it was necessary after 1839 to rent out jury rooms in town, so that the clerk of the superior court and the county court would have room to maintain records in the county building.

Things improved at Newnansville before cupidity struck it a deadly blow. In the 1850s workers set about erecting a new courthouse, and officials permitted a local man to move the old structure and two new jury rooms "provided that he remove and clean off all the rubbish and rotten stuff that may fall from taking them down." Just as prosperity seemed assured for the town, though, tragedy arrived in the form of the Florida Railroad. The route of David Yulee's proposed line lay through the nearby Hog Town area (soon to become Gainesville). Even as the new courthouse neared its completion on Newnansville's square in 1853, Alachua County voters opted to move the county seat to Gainesville. Yulee and local speculators saw more money for themselves and the railroad there, than they did at the former courthouse town. Eclipsed by the move, Newnansville eventually even lost its name, merging ultimately with the town of Alachua, itself a railroad development.[52]

Many clerks proved themselves to be remarkable and courageous individuals when confronted with challenges and crises such as these, and the following chapter will discuss several such men and their actions during the Civil War and Reconstruction. Sometimes, though, men with the best of intentions found themselves subjected to criticism at a time when ethical constraints were not so clearly drawn as at present.

One such man was Edmund Lee, first circuit court clerk of Manatee County (created in 1856). A Presbyterian minister by profession, Lee not only clerked but also operated as the only merchant in the tiny county seat village of Manatee (present-day Bradenton). Frail and small, yet full of energy, Lee was a visionary entrepreneur who also preached to blacks and evidenced a personality both amiable and eccentric: he once built a canal known as "Lee's Folly" that failed. His wife Electra, an excessive talker, taught school above Lee's store. She wore spectacles and whipped the legs of her students. County government in those days tended to take a relaxed attitude toward conflicts of interest, although some whistle blowers stood at the ready.

In any event, when Manatee County finally erected a courthouse at Manatee in 1859, Lee and others commanded attention. The building cost $700, and some residents hurled charges that, with Lee's connivance, it was unfairly contracted to one Ezekiel Glazier by the county commissioners. After all, Glazier held office as probate judge and ex-officio chairman of the board of commissioners. Besides, the Reverend Lee's house rested in view of the courthouse, he served on every jury, kept boarders who had county business, and, although it was irrelevant to the accusations, had his own boat and caught mullet which he sold. In any case, a one-story courthouse was built, although a lack of funds meant that lumber for the jail lay stacked neatly nearby and covered for future use. Through the Civil War the building served its purpose, but, as seen earlier in the chapter, by 1866 political retribution had resulted in relocation of the county seat miles to the east at Pine Level.[53]

Still and all, clerks often overcame any resentments they may have entertained about the demands placed upon them and reached out to assist other citizens. Fiscal affairs provided one area in which they constantly were called upon by others. In 1857, to provide one example, Marion County circuit clerk James Johnson demanded of state officials compensation for Robert Bulloch, the county jailer. The comptroller refused to pay Bulloch because of an administrative oversight by the previous sheriff. Johnson replied by demanding to know why Harris, Bulloch's replacement, received pay for his services. Johnson complained to the comptroller, "I have proposed to offer Mr. Bulloch's accounts precisely as Mr. Harris'[s] and still you say, `you can not audit the account.'" Johnson continued: "Now Sir, why you can allow this favoritism, I do not know, nor do I care--but I do say it's despicable in a public officer. I have but little more to say [but your favoritism] shall be showed in its true colors in every paper printed in the State of Florida."[54]

Beside the psychic pleasures of serving the public, what were the monetary rewards of clerks during the later territorial and early statehood period? The following schedule of fees for clerks of superior and county courts was enacted by the territorial council in 1832:

* *For entering appearance of defendant in person, or by attorney, six and a fourth cents.*
* *For docketing any cause on appearance docket, twelve and a half cents.*
* *For every Subpoena at law and return thereon, twenty-five cents.*
* *For every other process at law, or in chancery, or other legal proceeding, under seal of the court, with entry of return, fifty cents.*
* *Entry of every rule or order of court, twelve and a half cents.*
* *Administering oath, twelve and a half cents.*

* *Recording any order, proceeding, bill of sale, or other matter required to be recorded in a Book kept by said clerk for that purpose, per hundred words, fifteen cents.*
* *Copy of any certified paper, where the same shall not exceed one hundred words, eighteen and three fourth cents.*
* *Where the same shall exceed one-hundred words, for every hundred words, twelve and a half cents.*
* *For every search, twelve and a half cents.*
* *Entering judgment, twenty five cents.*
* *Drawing every advertisement, instructions attached to commissions for taking depositions, and all other papers, or writing, not herein otherwise provided for, where the same shall not exceed one hundred words, eighteen and three fourth cents.*
* *And, for every hundred words, more than one hundred, ten cents.*
* *For filing every paper, not process of court, six and a fourth cents.*
* *Swearing Jury, fifty cents.*
* *Recording mark and branch, twenty five cents.*[55]

Chapter 5

Through the Civil War

Florida officially organized itself as one of the United States on June 25, 1845, with the Tallahassee inauguration of Jefferson County lawyer and native North Carolinian William D. Moseley as governor. That event signaled the start of a tumultuous half-century-long era that would witness two bloody wars, sometimes-violent and bitterly divisive attempts at Republican Reconstruction and Bourbon Democrat Redemption, and a series of natural disasters that culminated in the devastating Great Freeze of 1895. In the process residents experienced what could be termed the birth of modern Florida, as the state's economy--particularly with the construction of railroads in the 1880s and 1890s--transformed itself amid explosive population increase. Through it all clerks of Florida's new circuit courts labored, sometimes at the risk of life or fortune, to execute the responsibilities with which the people and the law had intrusted them. Almost always they did so faithfully, but passions sometimes flared and, in isolated instances, oaths of trust and fidelity were violated.

The story of the first statehood-era clerks opened with the initial session of Florida's legislature, held at Tallahassee during the sweltering summer months of 1845. The legislative grind exposed raw political differences, as the lawmakers tackled their immense task. One participant summed up the experience for constituents by insisting that "It is no easy matter to organize a State Government."[56] Nonetheless, the process resulted in An Act to Organize the Circuit Courts, which implemented constitutional provisions scripted six-and-one-half years earlier at St. Joseph.[57]

The circuit court law contained provisions of particular interest and concern to court clerks and others anxious to hold a clerkship of the new trial court. Section 10 first provided that:

> *A Clerk of the Circuit Court shall be elected on the first Monday in October next in each county of this State wherein a Circuit Court is directed by law to be held, said election to be by qualified electors according to law; said Clerk to hold his office for the term of two years from the day of his election and until his successor is qualified; and said Clerk shall within thirty days after his election and before he enters on the duties of his office give bond in the penalty of two thousand dollars to the State of Florida, with two or more good sureties, to be approved by a Judge of one of the Circuit Courts or by the Solicitor of the Circuit in which said county is, and which bond shall be*

> *conditioned for the faithful discharge of the duties of his office.*[58]

The following section then established rules for transition from the old superior and county courts to the new circuit courts:

> *Until otherwise provided by law said Clerk shall receive the same fees for his official services as the Clerks of the Superior and County Courts of the Territory are respectively now allowed by law, and shall perform the same duties, have the same powers and be subject to like penalties, except such as the law of this State otherwise direct; and they shall use the Seal of court of the respective Superior Courts aforesaid as their seal of office.*[59]

In October 1845 spirited contests for clerkships clearly evidenced the interest taken locally in determining the person who would oversee and protect local records, as well as assist greatly in the administration of local judicial and executive affairs. Columbia County experienced a typical situation when former clerk Stirling Scarborough, a Whig, battled Democrat Levi Carter. Scarborough eventually bested his opponent, and one local man recalled the victor's first-day appearance in the new court, in the process reminding his readers that Florida in 1845 remained a poor state with its clerks often remaining in modest circumstances. "[Justice of the Peace Hugh G.] Hunter was very well dressed," remarked George G. Keen, "but S. Scarborough come in with his Sunday clothes on, for he didn't have any clothes but Sunday clothes, for he bought his every day clothes, and Sunday clothes off of the same piece, don't you see the point?" Columbia voters retained Scarborough as their clerk until his retirement in December 1857.[60]

For a single decade Florida's clerks enjoyed a peaceful opportunity to adapt to the new state of affairs before the calamities began to strike. Their accomplishments proved significant. "Florida's judicial system brought law, order, and civil authority to outlying settlements," concluded historian James M. Denham, "and judges and other court officials represented the state's most positive forces for unity."[61] One intriguing facet of the clerkship during that era involved the more-than-occasional election of Methodist ministers to the post, a tribute both to their education and to their need for employment that provided adequate compensation. Cotesworth L. Carruth, for instance, achieved election in October 1845 and served Madison County until 1850, when he remarried and moved to his new bride's properties in Columbia County.[62] Similarly, Oscar A. Myers administered affairs in Leon County from October 1849 to May 1852, before pursuing careers as preacher, lawyer, United States Attorney, newspaperman, and author.[63]

The calamities commenced in December 1855 when Indian war again beset Floridians. While fighting in this Third Seminole (or Billy Bowlegs) War confined itself to the central and southern peninsula, it disrupted affairs far more broadly. In an immediate sense, clerks in Manatee, Hillsborough, and Hernando counties prepared for the worse, but elsewhere courts experienced disruption and clerks endured added burdens as volunteer companies departed more-peaceful areas for campaigns in the south.[64]

Scarcely had Floridians recovered from the 1858 conclusion of Indian war before circumstances compelled them to face the national crisis of secession and Civil War. Florida departed from the Union on January 10, 1861, despite widespread opposition.[65] When secession convention members confronted former governor Richard Keith Call with the news, he voiced the fears of many. "And, what have you done?" he challenged. "You have opened up the gates of hell, from which shall flow the curses of the damned which shall sink you to perdition."[66]

Secession affected each clerk differently, although many heard the call to arms. Leon County's Council Bryan resigned on January 15, 1861, and by 1863 held rank as captain in the Fifth Florida Infantry (CSA). Polk County's Jehu J. Blount and Manatee County's John W. Whidden both served in the Seventh Florida.[67] Peter A. Crusoe experienced a more-complicated war. The Monroe County clerk first was deported by Union authorities from Key West, then the state's largest city. He joined the Confederate army, was taken prisoner at Tampa, was returned to Key West, and, "refusing to take the oath of allegiance," was kept in confinement for the duration. With the coming of peace, Crusoe then reassumed the powers of his office.[68]

Other clerks resisted the temptation to join the fighting and held on to their offices, which became an even-more-sought-after prize when the

Confederacy granted an exemption from the military draft in 1862 for incumbents of such local posts.[69] To continue functioning and to protect their records, several clerks were forced to take extraordinary measures. At Jacksonville, threatened with occupation in March 1862, officials buried some records and removed others westward to Lake City, which operated as a sort of county seat in exile for clerk Aaron W. DaCosta.[70]

David H. Higginbotham, who lived near Callahan, also buried Nassau County's records. A Union naval party arrested the clerk in January 1865 and demanded the public documents. Reported the party's commander: "The documents were hidden in the swamp, about one mile from his house, in a place which would have escaped detection without the aid of Mr. Higginbotham, who, I must say, acted in the most honorable manner, guiding the party through the woods to the boat by a much shorter route. He said he had always been a decided Union man."[71]

A clerk's office in exile served Escambia County, as well as Duval. With the Union capture of Pensacola only months away, the legislature in November 1861 approved a measure designating Filo E. de la Rua as circuit court clerk and as keeper of the Spanish Archives of the City of Pensacola. Unable to assume his duties until the evacuation was in progress, de la Rua discovered some of the records littering the floor of a local law office. He gathered and boxed everything and had the materials expressed to his home at Greenville, Alabama. The records remained there in de la Rua's custody until war's end. The clerk then carefully placed them in seventeen crates and returned them to Pensacola, where a United States Treasury Department agent accepted them on June 3, 1865.[72]

De la Rua's experience illustrates an additional problem endured by clerks during the war, that of adequate compensation for services rendered. Occupied counties obviously contributed nothing to support clerks in exile, and other counties were devastated by military raids, disease, scarcity, increasingly worthless currency, and other forces. In de la Rua's case, only a threat to resign brought a small measure of relief. "I have called a meeting of your Board [the Board of Aldermen of the City of Pensacola in exile at Greenville, Alabama]," a surviving letter of June 1864 declares, "to advise you that the City Treasurer, Mr. F. E. de la Rua has notified me that he is unwilling to serve as Keeper of the Archives, and a treasurer, for the compensation fixed by your Board at its late Session, via one hundred dollars per month."[73] The letter related only to de la Rua, but it spoke volumes of the trials of others.

At least one clerk faced immediate crisis that threatened his life and the safety of his family. The situation arose in Lafayette County in 1865, just as the Civil War neared its close. A mob of Union men and Confederate deserters raided the county seat of Old Troy, causing much damage. Tax assessor and clerk William Kinnon Jones, informed that the raiders planned another destructive attack, acted to save the county records. Aided by his thirteen-year-old daughter Rhoda, he moved the documents to his home on the edge of town. That night Old Troy, including the courthouse, was put to the torch. Nor did Jones escape the mob's wrath. The attackers fired his house and threatened to kidnap him. Finally, the blaze was doused and Jones was released, but the men confiscated his food, killed his chickens, and ran off his stock. Nonplused, the clerk kept his secret and saved the county records.[74]

One interesting account of Jones's actions was preserved by a local historian and provides tantalizing additional detail. Drawn from the memory of an aged citizen, it recounted the following tale:

> *At the time of the burning of the Troy courthouse, a one-legged man took the records from the courthouse because he had overheard men talking and knew they were planning to burn the courthouse. He was a farmer and had his cribs full of corn at the time. He hid the records underneath the corn. While the courthouse was burning the light was so bright that people living near it said they could read a newspaper by the blaze.*
>
> *After they were satisfied that the courthouse would burn down, they went to the house of the one-legged man for they had a suspicion he had hidden the records and they wanted them destroyed because some of them had criminal records they wished done away with. They knew the one-legged man kept the records for the county. They set fire to his house but when he came out and begged them to have mercy on him because he was crippled, they spared his corn crib. He looked so helpless they said they couldn't do such a dastardly thing to the crippled old man so they went back and put the fire out. Thus the records of Lafayette County were saved for future generations because of the bravery of a one-legged man.*[75]

By the time of the Lafayette County incident, the Civil War had taken an unspeakable toll on the state and its residents. While the Middle Florida plantation area for the most part had escaped serious damage, East and West Florida lay prostrate. Courts and schools had closed; businesses were bankrupted and shuttered; farms and homesteads in many areas smoldered; refugees huddled for warmth and pleaded for nourishment in primitive camps; and residents buried their dead and nursed their wounded with unbearable pain in the heart. At Tampa future Florida First Lady Catharine Hart echoed the sentiments of many by January of 1865. "Sometimes," she lamented to her family, "I am led to think God has forsaken us and intends to let us destroy each other."[76] Seemingly forsaken, Floridians awaited the coming of peace, unsure at all what it would mean to them.

Chapter 6

Reconstruction and Redemption

Floridians anxious for a return to peaceful conditions in the Civil War's aftermath discovered that their struggles only were beginning. Ahead of them awaited trials that would tear apart the social fabric of the state and open bitter wounds that, in some degree, have yet to heal. As this period of testing extended itself year after year, the focus of public attention and controversy often centered on the courts and the administration of local affairs. More than ever, circuit court clerks bore heavy responsibilities. A few faltered and others suffered heavy penalties, even to the loss of life. Yet, in this difficult era, men performed accomplishments difficult of achievement even in the best of times.

General Robert E. Lee's surrender at Appomattox Courthouse, Virginia, in April 1865, had foretold the Civil War's end in Florida, but the assassination of President Abraham Lincoln soon changed the direction of anticipated events. New President Andrew Johnson promulgated policies having the effect of placing most of the former Confederate states back into the hands of the South's prewar planter aristocracy. Once back in power, these men passed laws, known as Black Codes, that attempted to reinstate slavery in all but name. They also tolerated intimidation of Unionists and freedmen, with terror and bloodshed as results seen all too often.[77]

In the meantime state officials initiated efforts to reopen courts and courthouses which had closed during the war. Specifically, members of a constitutional convention held at Tallahassee in November 1865--one dominated by ex-Confederates--requested that Provisional Governor William Marvin permit civil officials who had held office prior to the surrender to take up their duties once again. With some exceptions, Marvin responded by directing the officers, including circuit court clerks, to carry on as they had previously. The experience of Monroe County's Peter A. Crusoe offers one example. The former secessionist, as mentioned earlier, simply stepped out of Union confinement and back into his office at Key West.[78]

That many Rebels held clerkships and circuit judgeships caused very real problems for Unionists in some counties, when they were denied access

to the courts. As one United States official reported in mid-1867, "The Civil Courts will not entertain suits for damages for the taking of property during the war." He continued: "A case was recently brought before the Circuit Court of Polk Co. and was thrown out by the Judge. Other cases were to be brought before the Circuit Court in Manatee County, but for some cause the Court did not meet, notwithstanding that the Law Requires the Judge to hold Court on the fourth Monday in April." Ironically, the judge, Tampa's James Gettis, was a northerner by birth, something he shared in common with many of the state's most-ardent secessionists.[79]

From Washington, the Congress permitted the worsening situation in the South to continue only until the spring of 1867, when its members enacted a series of statutes called the Military Reconstruction acts. The laws effectively mandated the grant of voting rights to adult freedmen and compelled the rewriting of state constitutions under the authority of military governors. Republican administrations thereafter exercised power in most of the southern states for varying periods up to eight or nine years.[80]

Floridians witnessed the beginning implementation of this Reconstruction revolution during a constitutional convention convened at the state capitol during January and February 1868. The majority-white gathering nonetheless was dominated by Republicans, but party adherents split into warring camps over the specifics of designing a government and ensuring rights of residents. At one point the political sparring resulted in a withdrawal of more-moderate members, who afterward secretly returned to the capitol and seized control of the convention.

The compromises necessary to ensure conservative support for the moderate group's constitution deprived voters of the opportunity to elect their own circuit court clerks, as well as most other local officials. Conservatives, particularly those in the black-majority counties of the Middle Florida plantation belt, feared black control of local government. To assuage them, the constitution drafters conferred upon the governor power to appoint all local officials except for constables, legislators, and municipal officers. They retained circuit courts, but also reinstituted the old county courts for misdemeanor trials and minor civil actions.[81]

Regarding circuit clerks, the Constitution of 1868 specified at Article VI, Section 19, broad authority and a lengthened term. The provision read, in part:

> *The Governor, by and with the advice and consent of the Senate, shall appoint in each county a . . . Clerk of the Circuit Court, who shall also be Clerk of the County Court and Board of County Commissioners, Recorder, and ex-officio Auditor of the county, each of whom shall hold his office for four years. Their duties shall be prescribed by law.*[82]

Republican Governor Harrison Reed and a Republican legislature assumed control of state affairs during the summer of 1868 and immediately acted to specify the duties of circuit clerks. The series of statutes detailed responsibilities and set fees, taking particular care to instruct clerks on their

Photograph courtesy of the Florida State Archives.

Andrew Jackson served as military govenor for Florida from March 10, to October 8, 1821, when he resigned. Despite his brief tenure, Jackson exercised a profound influence on Florida as both a territory and a state.

Photograph courtesy of the St. Augustine Historical Society.

The Spanish Provost Guard House was used as the first territorial courthouse for St. John's County (established July 21, 1821).

Photograph courtesy of the Florida State Archives.

Robert Meacham was the illegitimate son of a slave and a white planter. He became Florida's first black circuit clerk when he was appointed to that position for Jefferson County in 1868.

Photograph courtesy of the Florida State Archives.

Samuel Pasco, Confederate veteran and future United States Senator, served as circuit clerk for Jefferson County immediately after the Civil War.

duties regarding elections and criminal prosecutions. They represented an updating and comprehensive treatment previously unseen on Florida's lawbooks. Given the constitutional mandate and these new laws, clerks emerged as potentially the most-powerful officials of local government.[83]

Buttressed with enhanced constitutional and legal authority, a new cadre of clerks assumed power thanks to Reed's appointments. Most were Republicans, and, eventually, at least three were blacks. The first freedman appointed was Robert Meacham of Jefferson County, whom Reed placed in office in August 1868. The son of Banks Meacham--who had served in the 1838-1839 constitutional convention--and one of his slaves, Robert Meacham had represented Jefferson County in the 1868 constitutional convention and sat in the state senate from 1868 to 1879. In a political dispute a few months after the appointment, Reed attempted to force Meacham from the senate, but the lawmaker chose instead to resign his clerkship. At the time a Jacksonville newspaper sympathized with his dilemma. "The Clerkship is a profitable office, more so than the Senatorship," noted the *Florida Union*, "and so far as Mr. Meacham's personal interests are concerned, it is for his advantage to keep it."[84]

Meacham's 1868 appointment stirred controversy and provoked incumbent Jefferson County clerk Samuel Pasco to protest, an incident that well illustrates the tender emotions of the times. When confronted by Meacham, Pasco--a one-time Confederate soldier and future United States senator--angrily recorded his sentiments in the circuit court order book. He wrote:

> *Be it remembered that on 24 August, 1868 came Robert Meacham and claimed the office of Clerk of the Court by virtue of a certain instrument purporting to be a commission from one Harrison Reed claiming to be Governor of the State . . . and it appearing that the said H. R. is actually exercising the functions of Governor . . . and that he has full power to enforce the said Commission, the undersigned, believing it to be his duty as a good citizen to yield obedience to the existing government has this day surrendered all the records, seals and other public property that has been in his custody as Clerk of the Circuit and Criminal Courts in and for this county of Jefferson to the said Robert Meacham, but he does the same under protest reserving and claiming all his rights as Clerk as aforesaid. And he protests the authority under which the said Robert Meacham is acting is unlawful and a usurpation.*[85]

Over two years passed after Meacham's resignation before Reed again turned to an African American to hold a clerk's office. Then, in February 1871 he named Pennsylvania-born Henry S. Harmon to the clerkship for Alachua County, a position that the lawyer and Union army veteran held until February 1873. Harmon had served during 1868-1870 in the Florida House of Representatives and from 1873 to 1875 would act as that body's clerk. Seven months after Harmon's designation, Reed turned to a New York native and teacher, John C. Gambia, to execute the clerk's responsibilities in Madison County. Thirty years old at the time of his appointment, Gambia held the position until April 1874.[86]

The Reconstruction period, begun amid bitter tensions, soon turned openly violent in a number of areas, with personal consequences for some clerks. In February 1869, for instance, state senator William J. Purman and Jackson County circuit clerk Dr. John L. Finlayson attended a minstrel show at Marianna. After the performance, while they were crossing a street, an assassin blasted the two men with shotgun fire, wounding Purman and killing Finlayson. The shooting was the first in a string of murderous incidents known to history as the Jackson County War. It probably also was the first instance of a Florida circuit clerk being murdered while in office, at least for political reasons.[87]

By 1876--given various scandals, quarrels between factions, political violence, and disillusionment--Republicans faced the likelihood of loosing control of Florida government to Democrats. In the circumstances, the clerkship of one county played a major role in an attempt to deny some Democrats the chance to vote. Manatee County clerk John F. Bartholf fell ill and resigned. Then, local Republican leader James D. Green proposed to Governor Marcellus Stearns an intriguing ploy: appoint my son Andrew as clerk but we will delay executing the necessary bond, leaving the county without a clerk and forcing cancellation of elections. Stearns agreed and set the plan in motion. Meanwhile, Manatee Democrats demanded voting lists, which Andrew Green refused to provide. Irate, the Democrats called a rump election and cast 289 ballots for their gubernatorial candidate George F. Drew. The two parties then indulged in a passionate and prolonged quarrel about the election's final tally, with returns from several counties in dispute. Finally, the state supreme court, with a Republican majority, ordered officials to include Manatee's rump election returns in their totals, giving the statehouse to the Democrats and ending Reconstruction in Florida.[88]

The advent of Democratic rule in early 1877 was called by Democrats at the time and by historians subsequently as the Redemption, imparting the almost-Messianic emotionalism that surrounded the event. Given the intensity of feelings on all sides, it is not surprising that Governor Drew acted immediately to replace local officers, mostly Republicans and many African Americans, with loyal Democrats. The ax fell so quickly and so hard that at least one prominent newspaper labeled its stories of the transition with the title, "The Guillotine," which it complemented with the subtitle, "Republicans Requested to Scoot, While Democrats Waltz Joyfully up to Serve and Save the Country."[89]

If some Republicans had used the office of circuit clerk as a political instrument, Democrats proceeded to do the same. Fortunately, most of the newcomers to the office of clerk entered upon their duties soberly and acted with responsibility. A small number, though, permitted partisan passions to lead them into embarrassing and illegal chicanery. Once again, the frontier county of Manatee offers an excellent illustration. There, Democratic leaders apparently attempted political retribution on county Republican leader James D. Green, likely for his role in attempting to block the 1876 elections. Abetting them, clerk John G. Spottswood manipulated the grand jury list so as to pack the panel with Green's enemies. The jury, in turn, indicted the former Union army captain and legislator on trumped up charges.[90]

The Democratic scheme worked well until a local resident revealed the plot in a letter to a Key West newspaper. In the resulting embroglio, Democrats--including future governor Henry L. Mitchell and future congressman Stephen M. Sparkman--focused blame on Spottswood, who was forced to resign in exchange for not being prosecuted. The anger stimulated by the affair soon passed away, as Florida's chronic problem with land titles re-emerged as the key public issue. As one Manatee resident put it in a letter to the Tampa *Guardian*, "In fact the lands are in as great a muddle, as the Clerk's Office; but the clerk has now gone where the `woodbine twineth' and left a clear field for us all to put in our `Cuss Finger.'"[91]

On the other hand, efforts of Redeemer officials to enforce the law to protect Republicans and punish malefactors occasionally placed clerks and their employees in jeopardy. A case in point originated in Hernando County in 1877. On June 26, the Reverend Arthur St. Clair, an African American who previously had held office as county voter registrar and county commissioner, was gunned down following a political gathering. A mass meeting of county whites condemned the murder, declaring:

> That we do, on behalf of ourselves, our county and State, denounce this and all violations of the criminal law as disgraceful and heinous, and that it is our duty as such citizens to detect and bring to condign punishment the disturbers of our peace and violators of our law. That we hold equally guilty, with the perpetrators of this crime, whether resident in this

county or not, any person who may know the names of the murderers and not make them known to the officers of the law.[92]

Pursuant to the meeting's call, Hernando County's officials, including the circuit court clerk, set about collecting evidence to identify and convict the assassins. By September they had narrowed the culprits to members of a prominent family and stored the evidence in the courthouse (likely the clerk's office) for safekeeping preliminary to the approaching session of the circuit court. Then, in early October, the killers struck back, as they or their associates burned the courthouse in order to destroy the evidence held against them. The act brought to public attention the names of the suspected persons. One newspaper account described the county, at the time, as being "In Chaos," but the airing of the names may well have saved the lives of those such as the clerk who knew the information in the destroyed documents.[93]

While Democrats ruled Florida after 1876, Republicans black and white attempted repeatedly to challenge Bourbon power for over a decade, sometimes in cooperation with disaffected Democrats. In the early 1880s the "Independent" movement especially evidenced the potential for such an alliance. It, in turn, prompted the Redeemers, as the Bourbons also were called, to move ahead with plans to write and adopt a new state constitution to buttress their popularity and initiate new efforts to eliminate their opposition from the voting booth. As a result, during the summer of 1885 a constitutional convention of eighty-two Democrats, twenty-three Republicans (seven of whom were African Americans), and three Independents convened at Tallahassee.[94]

As had occurred at each past convention, the role of clerks of the circuit court and, particularly, their method of selection held an important position in the convention debates. Especially, some delegates led by Hernando County's Austin S. Mann demanded local election of all local officers, reflecting the old spirit of Jacksonian Democracy and requiring substantial change from the Constitution of 1868's provision for appointment by the governor.[95] Black Duval County delegate Thomas V. Gibbs, the son of one-time Florida secretary of state and superintendent of public instruction Jonathan C. Gibbs, explained the situation:

> *It was the avowed intention of the Democrats in calling the convention, while placing as far as possible the powers of government in the hands of the people, to restrict as much as might be done the influence of the colored vote in that government. Under the pretense of "protecting the black belt," which comprises the wealthiest and most populous counties in the State, it was proposed to so manipulate matters as to keep these counties, though heavily Republican, out of Republican hands. The manner in which this was proposed to be done was (1) by imposing a poll-tax to be made a pre-requisite to the right to vote; (2) by keeping the election machinery out of the hands of the hands of the people; (3) by certain restrictions on official bonds.*
>   *This was the plan of the Bourbons, most of whom reside in the "black belt" counties, and who delight in calling themselves the "best element." Opposed to them were the liberal Democrats, composed largely of Northern men, many of whom were Republicans in the North but who, driven by the color-line into the Democratic party, yet hold certain principles of fair play and self-preservation above party dictation. After a tedious fight of nearly two months the result of the convention was a compromise. The Bourbons got the circuit Judges and*

> *County Commissioners appointive, thus saving their election machinery, and the Liberals succeeded in having the Supreme Bench, county Judges[, clerks of the circuit court,] and Justices of the Peace made elective.*[96]

The compromise also diminished somewhat the constitutional stature of the clerk's office, by leaving the delineation of most of its responsibilities to the legislature. The language provided at Article XI, Section 30:

> *The Clerk of said Court shall be elected by the electors of the county in which the Court is held and shall hold his office for four years and his compensation shall be fixed by law. He shall also be Clerk of the County Court. The Sheriff of the County shall be executive officer of said Court and his duties and fees shall be fixed by law.*[97]

Voters approved the new constitution at elections held in 1886, setting the stage for the first general election of clerks and certain other local officials in Florida since the beginning of the Reconstruction era. Mostly Democrats won, but a few counties elected Republicans. In one county, Duval, voters chose Republican Joseph E. Lee, an African American and former representative and senator, as clerk. Apparently, though, Lee was unable to secure an appropriate bond and never received his commission. Subsequent elections virtually guaranteed Democrats all such offices. The period since 1885 had witnessed a new challenge to that party, as black Republicans and the Knights of Labor organization had combined to grasp power in a number of towns and cities. In reaction the 1889 legislature adopted a poll tax that, effectively, drove most poor people, black and white, away from the ballot, ensuring easy Democratic majorities thereafter.[98]

Florida's political wars of Reconstruction and Redemption, though of crucial importance, masked fundamental changes in the state, its economy, and its society. Railroad and hotel construction spurred by magnates such as William D. Chipley, Henry M. Flagler, and Henry B. Plant, together with the activities of large-scale developers such as Hamilton Disston, brought hundreds of thousands of newcomers. Whether tourist or settler, these visitors and emigrants brought a far-more-complex life to the one-time frontier state. In the process, clerks of the circuit court faced ever-greater challenges as Florida proceeded posthaste into the Twentieth Century.[99]

Chapter 7

Responsibilities Fulfilled--
And The Future

Florida's clerks were challenged by the responsibilities they faced--both as to number and complexity--as the United States moved from 1900 through the next 100 years. What would the twentieth century hold for the clerks, and were there generalizations that could be made about them? By the 1970s Florida's clerks and their staff performed 926 constitutional and statutory tasks, and, in the late 1990s, merely listing their duties required sixteen single-spaced pages of manuscript. In the decade of the 1970s, two scholars, Larry Berkson and Steven Hays, made a preliminary assessment of their role. Berkson and Hays agreed that the circuit clerks had remained key elements of local government, but they additionally found that a proper analysis of their place and importance had yet to be accomplished.[100]

The primary reason so little was known, the Berkson and Hays study showed, was that clerks had been ignored by scholars. But why? They had been overlooked, in part, because the very title of "clerk" seemed mundane. In fact, it was derived from the Latin <u>clericus</u>, meaning clergyman, and thus a learned person capable of performing demanding tasks. Despite the historical context, to Americans the term "clerk" implied a lackluster position and did not command respect. Further lack of recognition came because the clerk's role was low profile. They rarely made headlines. No dramatic decisions involving life or death, freedom or imprisonment were involved in the job. Nor did the official have the legislative power of county commissioners who controlled road locations and construction, waste management facilities, and other services. Many people saw the clerk as essentially a non-political person. Yet Berkson and Hays correctly asserted that the clerk was an important political figure even though the position's responsibilities were administrative. The clerk was and is an elected official and must by definition be a politician in order to remain in office. By the 1970s when local courts commanded scholarly attention, the symbiotic relation of clerks to the judicial system attracted attention to them as well, and beyond that, to their other work.

Berkson and Hays saw Florida clerks as diverse individuals involved in both executive and judicial duties and noted that the dichotomy could produce conflicts. The revelation was news perhaps to citizens unacquainted with local government, but to the clerks themselves the situation was a part of their historical heritage. They contended that their independence as constitutionally elected officials enhanced the concept and implementation of the principle of checks and balances. Their constitutional position as popularly chosen officials insured that neither judges nor county commissions could fire them. Without question, their broad authority gave them a position of power, but, unless wisely used, their power would make county government unworkable and, pragmatically considered, result in an officious clerk being voted out of office.

Clerks viewed themselves and their work as embodying the essence of democratic government, a continuance of Jacksonian concepts of rule by the people. To the argument that having an elective officer serve as an administrator was unwise because it made the officer place reelection ahead of administrative efficiency, clerks replied that fairness plus management capabilities and effectiveness were what kept them in office. Advocates of maintaining the circuit clerk insisted that the office was one of public trust, and the public should decide who held it.

Berkson and Hays produced research that enabled them to draw some conclusions about Florida's circuit clerks. They observed that clerks came to office at an earlier age than judges or county commissioners and served for longer periods. Their knowledge of county government and what could and could not be done in their county was more extensive than that of any other officer. The typical circuit judge or county commissioner was dependent upon the clerk who, taken in the larger context, was probably the single most-important county official. Twentieth-century clerks tended to be well educated and those since World War II even more so.

One problem, which requires on-going attention, has been the clerks' lack of formal management training. Their education, no matter how extensive, begins rather than ends with election to office. Effective management and budgetary techniques, computer technology, and data processing require increased training by clerks and their personnel. Circuit clerks have their share of problems with the legislature--including lack of understanding by senators and representatives, poorly written laws that are difficult to interpret, laws that require rapid change, and obtaining reporting forms that are uniform and consistent. Those concerns may be coupled with ambiguous and inconsistent directions from judges, not to mention fiscal ambiguities, administrative policy questions, and personality clashes derived from their work with county commissioners. To be a good circuit clerk is to be able to cope, to compromise, and to face problems that call for receptivity to change, innovation, and flexibility. Never enough time, usually not enough space, inadequate equipment, and chronic questions of sufficient finances are all issues that must be considered. Historically, circuit clerks have sometimes fallen far short of the lofty standards their position demands. Yet the men and women who hold the job agree that, despite the bottomless barrel of detail and special pleading, the clerk's pervading thought must not be of power but of service--to all the people.[101]

Clearly, the clerks operated in a state that changed dramatically in a century, and, consciously and unconsciously, they were affected by those larger events. Florida was transformed from one of the less-populous states to a position of fourth in the nation by the 1990s. Over 14 million Floridians awaited the new millennium. When Florida became a state in 1845, it held 69,000 people. In 1860 it boasted slightly over 140,000 residents, and most of them lived in the northern counties. What remained was not merely rural, it was frontier, a vast peninsula of woods, water, and wilderness. Still, determined people, roads and rails, and the luck of geography that made possible agricultural riches already had combined to place Florida in an advantageous position by 1900.

Moore good fortune in the form of changing lifestyles would make Florida unique in the South. Climate and unrivaled beaches became irresistible allures and, later, automobiles (plus airplanes) and air conditioning proved that distance could be conquered and the calendar provided with artificial seasons. Along with its traditional assets of timber, agriculture, and livestock, Florida became the beneficiary of the twentieth-century's on-going technological revolution.[102]

Population expansion mirrored all these changes. From slightly over half-a-million people in 1900, the state followed a growth pattern that was moderate in the century's first two decades, exploded in the 1920s, and slowed during the years of the Great Depression. It accelerated during World War II and the last half of the 1940s, only to surge even-more-dramatically in the twentieth century's remaining decades. The statistics listed below demonstrate the numerical changes:

Florida's Population 1900-1990

	Total	White	Black
1900	528,542	297,333	230,730
1910	752,619	443,636	308,609
1920	968,470	638,153	329,487
1930	1,468,211	1,035,205	431,828
1940	1,897,414	1,381,986	514,198
1950	2,771,305	2,166,051	603,101
1960	4,951,560	4,063,881	808,186
1970	6,789,383	5,724,464	1,041,535
1980	9,746,324	8,184,855	1,343,134
1990	12,937,926	10,749,285	1,759,534[103]

With increased population came new counties, with the greatest demographic changes occurring in the state's southern region. More people meant more structural changes in county government, and that meant additional county officials, including the circuit clerks. Of the state's present sixty-seven counties, twenty-two were established between 1909 and 1925: Palm Beach (1909), Pinellas (1911), Bay (1913), Seminole (1913), Broward (1915), Okaloosa (1915), Flagler (1917), Okeechobee (1917), Hardee (1921), Highlands (1921), Charlotte (1921), Glades (1921), Dixie (1921), Sarasota (1921), Union (1921), Collier (1923), Hendry (1923), Martin (1925), Indian River (1925), Gulf (1925), and Gilchrist (1925). Only three of the new counties (Bay, Okaloosa, and Gulf) were in the Panhandle to the northwest. Flagler and Union lay in the northeast, while Dixie and Gilchrist were located in the north-central region. The remaining fifteen were in south Florida.[104]

No new counties were added after 1925, as demographic changes took the form of rapid population growth in urban areas. Once again, the state's southern sections took a strong lead. In the twentieth century's last decades, northern counties also saw their populations increase. The circuit clerks there made, and are making, adjustments similar to those previously accomplished in south Florida. Besides the increase of population by native-born Floridians and Americans, south Florida (and increasingly central and even north Florida) experienced an enormous expansion of Hispanic-American population, especially those immigrants seeking asylum from Castro's Cuba. Since the Cubans first came in substantial numbers after 1959, the state has moved through time to become a multi-cultural entity, far more ethnically and linguistically diverse than any other southern state. That the sheer cost of operating the state and its counties and the attendant social tensions of multi-culturalism--a complicated and changing population stir of African Americans, Caribbean-Latin Americans, Mexicans, and whites--has created new responsibilities for clerks and increasing demands upon them is undeniable.[105]

Even earlier, clerks were witness to and saw their jobs reflect the changing roles of blacks in twentieth-century society: black population rose as its members, along with whites, experienced industrialization, World War I, the boom of the 1920s, the Great Depression of the 1930s, World War II, and post-war expansion. Yet, during those epochs and upheavals, blacks' economic, political, and social experiences were those of second-class citizens. Sometimes they were far worse, as exampled by the race-based murders at Rosewood in 1923 that claimed eight lives. By the 1950s the demands of African Americans for an equitable place in society could be begrudged but not denied by the United States searching for a legitimate and powerful place as the leader of world democracy. The painful struggles for blacks that followed the *Brown* decision of 1954 (overturning legal segregation of public education in existence since the *Plessy* case in 1896) were inevitably addressed by circuit clerks on a day-to-day basis. Segregation in private and public life, including, as the clerks well knew, previous court and other legal restrictions, fell.[106]

Florida politics evolved as the state's complexion changed. In 1900 and as a result primarily of legal strictures, the state's 230,730 blacks had a political voice so small that it was difficult to measure. Their world was still

Jim Crow in 1944: Florida had only about 20,000 black voters (many Republicans since the Democrats excluded them from party membership). By 1992, though, the state claimed 521,328 black voters, and they influenced elections from those of circuit clerks and other local races to national contests. Backed by federal court rulings, federal laws, and belated state statutes, Florida officials and their constituents entered a new era. It was one where the state, itself, could address problems not obfuscated by the old and crippling issues of race and segregation.

Of the various governmental changes that followed, the new constitution of 1968 was one of the most important. The long-needed document made reapportionment (order by the federal supreme court in 1967) a reality and revamped the old constitution of 1885. In general, the document strengthened the governor (he could serve two consecutive terms, had budgetary responsibilities, and more control as executive departments were consolidated). On the other hand, the new constitution retained the cabinet system, which continued to divide executive authority. The charter-- together with the Legislative Reorganization Act of 1969, which led to annual sessions of the lawmakers, and the creation of permanent legislative staffs-- left the state legislature with adequate strength to insure that the separation of powers concept was still in effect.[107]

The new charter, despite advances, created concerns for Florida's circuit clerks. They worried that the new constitution's local government section might eliminate their administrative relationships with county commissions. Additionally, strong sentiment existed among some Floridians to increase local autonomy through the expedient of charter government, and clerks feared the loss of their constitutional status as elected officials.

The thrust for the growing home rule movement was national in scope and went back to the nineteenth century, when some form of expanded local authority was adopted in Iowa and Missouri. By the 1950s in Florida, as elsewhere, the feeling was that the old idea of counties (the thinking applied generally to municipalities as well) as subdivisions of the state was wrong and impeded effective government. The argument was that the legislature wasted too much time with special legislation for counties that could be better used on statewide issues. Further, counties and cities were far more than appendages of the state, having their own particular concerns and problems, and local people should control them as much as possible. Counties did not need, the argument went, the long delays brought about by obtaining special permission from the state to address local matters. In general, the idea was to free up the busy legislature and to give the county electorate greater control.[108]

The argument for increased autonomy for counties and cities had greater logical appeal in heavily populated urban counties, and in 1956 Dade County became the first in the state to become a charter county. Since there was no constitutional provision for such a switch, a special amendment was approved and added to the 1885 document. It vested powers of limited home rule (a precedent that would be followed with future charter counties), and

Dade was still bound by the 1885 constitution and the state's general laws. Dade continued to be Florida's only charter county prior to the constitution of 1968.[109]

The experiment in Dade County was felt throughout the state. Yet, a simpler method than passing a special constitutional amendment for each county desiring to adopt a charter was needed. The time was ripe for action, as a reform atmosphere was compelling lawmakers to address numerous issues of public concern. For example, Florida's climate of change encompassed legislative reapportionment and redistricting (prompted by federal court orders) and ideas for institutionalizing "government in the sunshine" as promulgated by then-state senator Lawton Chiles and others. At about the same time, the drafting of a new constitution modernizing and recasting Florida government presented an opportunity for charter county enthusiasts. On their part, circuit clerks were not averse to extending local rule but believed that it could be done within the traditional framework of elected constitutional officers and by retaining the principles of election by the people and other checks and balances.

As the circuit clerks hoped, the constitution makers in 1968 retained the Jacksonian concept of popular election, thus preserving checks and balances. Still, they demonstrated a responsive attitude toward more home rule and devised a streamlined means of accomplishing that end. They also went further by authorizing the state to expand the powers of local government by statute. Article VIII, Section 1(c) gave each county the right to establish a charter government that was to be adopted, amended, or repealed only by the voters in a county in a special election. This was the first time in Florida history that counties were uniformly permitted to establish charter governments. In theory and practice, citizens would have the power to form a county plan more responsible to their needs. Such counties were more powerful than counties with traditional forms of government.

County government by charter encountered difficulties, as its critics, including circuit clerks and their organization (the Florida Association of Court Clerks and Comptrollers) had predicted. Inevitable problems included charter provisions that were in conflict with the state constitution, state statutes, and municipal ordinances. Opponents argued that they created additional bureaucracies; were not necessary, particularly in smaller counties; and eliminated traditional elected officers--such as clerks--and, by doing so, frustrated the time-honored and proven idea of checks and balances.[110]

The authors of the constitution also addressed the judiciary article, but in 1970 a separate amendment lacking in essential reforms met with rejection by Florida voters. Then, another judiciary article was offered to the electorate for its consideration in 1972 that contained more-ambitious reform ideas.[111] Circuit clerks once again feared that changes would eliminate their status within the court system. They closely monitored the proceedings. The clerks correctly anticipated a major overhaul of Article V.

As one scholar has written, "The 1972 revision plainly transferred power from the legislature to the judiciary by depriving the legislature of the power to organize and administer the courts, to prescribe rules of practice and procedure, and to prescribe rules of attorney admission and discipline."[112]

While the changes diminished the power of the legislature, they recast the duties of the circuit clerks so as to increase their powers and responsibilities. More than ever, they were bound to the judiciary. After the Constitution of 1968 and adoption of the judicial article revision in 1972, popularly elected clerks remained very much an essential part of local government in Florida.[113]

Despite the care with which constitutions are drafted, inevitably areas of confusion arise. Changes regarding county government and the roles of circuit clerks naturally have received judicial attention. In an important case decided in 1977, the Supreme Court of Florida heard an appeal from Alachua County that held local and statewide ramifications. The case came when A. Curtis Powers, circuit clerk of Alachua County, sought clarification of his fiscal duties as clerk of the county commission in four capacities: as auditor, accountant, custodian, and investor of county funds. The court upheld the lower circuit court in most particulars. In effect it clarified ambiguities about the circuit clerk's constitutional authority over budget preparation and administrative duties, in a situation where the county commission was attempting to transfer them to the county administrator. As the high tribunal determined, the circuit clerk, in the absence of special legislation to the contrary, was the county's chief fiscal officer. A similar case, pending in the late 1990s, had sparked further debate and promised additional consideration of the issue.[114]

Florida's circuit clerks find their lives touched by the many technical demands placed upon them, but they know that, in the larger sense, what they do affects not just administrative politics but education, the environment, roads, water, crime, medical and social needs, the elderly, children, the poor, and a myriad of concerns that impact society. Failure to address these issues is to accept the blessings of democracy, while ignoring its obligations. For a circuit clerk, such a situation would be intolerable.

Who then are these individuals who serve Florida as their circuit clerks? How have they changed during the present century and how, in turn, have those changes affected the clerk's role? To answer those questions, a personal glimpse is in order. That glimpse may be found in Chapter VIII.

Chapter 8

Tradition and Diversity: Facing the Challenges of the Modern Era

As Florida has undergone dramatic changes during the twentieth century, so too have the difficulties faced by clerks of the circuit court, as well as the characteristics of the clerks, themselves. Sometimes tradition rooted deeply in office and county have anchored the institution and its operations, while other times newfound diversity has provided keys to greater understanding and new directions. Given the cooperative efforts of and continuing interchanges among Florida's clerks, old lessons remembered and new lessons learned have spread to benefit all counties as they have plunged ahead into the truly challenging modern era.

Madison County's clerk Tim Sanders, interviewed in his courthouse office in 1996, offered a case study as to how, on a personal level, the position can constitute an anchor of continuity for county residents amid the bureaucratic sea of increasingly complex and impersonal government. He was first elected clerk in his own right in 1992, but his direct ties with the office and people of Madison County are much more profound. At least three of his family members have preceded him in the clerk's position, including Leighton Maynard Perry (1865-1867), James Porter Perry (1887-1895), and Thomas Zachariah Martin (1895-1912). Apparently clerking runs in the family blood, as Sanders' great-great-great-great-grandfather, John Perry, presided as a county clerk in South Carolina at least as early as 1796. Because his ancestral roots run so deep, what happens in Madison necessarily is of abiding concern to Sanders. He takes an active and meaningful part in the community's social and civic life. His goals encompass much more than the emoluments of public office, and they form a bridge of continuity between the past and the present.[115]

In a growth state such as Florida, stability in public office is not only something to be desired by an incumbent, but it also represents an asset that often provides real benefits for the electorate--so long as the service is efficient, honest, and respondent to the community's needs. By definition or by fact, few offices exceed that of circuit clerk in touching the lives of the populace. Having people in office with community ties and concerns for local people can provide psychological comfort and actual support, achievements that can be measured by clerks' dedication and real services performed.

The personal experiences of clerks other than Tim Sanders illustrate these truths, and listening to Ernie Lee Magaha speak in 1996 proved particularly enlightening. Magaha is circuit clerk of Escambia County in the rapidly growing Pensacola area, where a still-rural culture is in the historic process of becoming urbanized and is inevitable heir to the comforts and discomforts of growth. As in the rest of the South, white men such as Magaha have traditionally held most of Florida's circuit clerkships, even though, as will be seen, modern democratic changes have reduced their predominance. Despite the changes, Magaha's talk of mounting complexities, ever-increasing demands, and innovative approaches provided a primer in survival techniques for clerks grounded in tradition and experience. More than that, it was a statement of the need for common sense and a reasonable attitude toward the circuit clerk's office, the staff members who share the work load, and those fellow county residents whom they serve.

Magaha's individual story added depth and nuance to the lessons he imparted, and, while intensely personal, it speaks as well for other circuit clerks. Certainly, his success is difficult to argue with--he was elected in 1956 in a three-man race and has held office to the present with scarcely a challenge, threatened or real. He is such a veteran of office that he can recall vividly the continuing use of quill pens as of the time he first took his oath of office. His achievements take on particular luster when examined against a backdrop of population changes, the rise of the two-party system in Florida, the civil rights era, constitutional reorganization, expanding responsibilities, and exponential technological change.

Without question and as Magaha's experience shows, balancing the requirements of a circuit clerk as chief fiscal officer for the county, <u>ex-officio</u> to the board of county commissioners, and clerk of the court (to mention only the most demanding duties) calls for special skills, often the product of background and temperament. In Magaha's case, the story began at Jay, Florida, where he was born and continued in the Escambia County town of Century where he attended high school. The young man then served in the army for eighteen months before returning to pursue studies in business at Auburn University. Following graduation he settled in Pensacola and eventually entered politics. Once elected clerk, he adjusted by formulating an approach that worked effectively. According to the clerk, a personal touch is required. He employs a "hands on style," and, as he put it, he and his staff serve the people, aware of their duty to act as an audience and be "good neighbors." He said, "I've never wanted a talking machine atmosphere." For him, "the office belongs to the people" and, properly nowadays, the "people expect more and demand more." Magaha has established as a major guideline that "humility is a sign of strength of character." The staff is so aware of their public role that they conduct seminars even on telephone etiquette.

Neither Magaha nor his staff seeks confrontation with judges, and, like other circuit court operations in Florida, they "try to avoid practicing law." In their relations with county commissioners, the clerk and his personnel "don't try to second guess." As he puts it: "We're low key. We don't pick out issues." Substituted for such issue involvement is emphasis on hard work in making the machinery of government turn on a day-to-day basis. "Population in Florida has just exploded," Magaha explained. "If you relax one day, you get behind." His staff members go through annual evaluations in which they rate their own performance. The office benefits from a high degree of loyalty derived from policies that encourage individual initiative, mutual trust, and flexibility. Magaha practices "not looking over their shoulders." His personnel are free to work both as individuals and closely together. Even so, the clerk realizes what all circuit clerks discover sooner or later: they, themselves, are ultimately responsible. "I'm in charge of the store," he says.[116]

The offices conducted by men such as Sanders and Magaha are well-run, white, male-directed operations, but their basic procedures typify those followed by all clerks regardless of race or gender. Yet, increasingly women and blacks have come to hold the position of clerk, and their story also is an important part of history and the evolution of broadbased democracy in Florida.

Regarding the emergence of women, Florida's path to the voting booth and public office proved a tortuous one. Only after a long struggle and the adoption of the nineteenth amendment to the federal constitution in 1920 did the state's women enjoy rights of suffrage, this despite the fact that Florida's legislature did not ratify the amendment until 1969. Nonetheless, Florida women enjoyed guaranteed voting rights as of 1920 and began to play an active role in politics.[117]

Toward the end of the 1920s, women were being elected to various state and local offices in increasing numbers, with the year 1928 setting important precedents. That year, for example, Mamie Eaton Greene of Monticello achieved election to the Railroad Commission and became the first woman to hold statewide office. The same year, Edna Giles Fuller of Orlando became the first woman elected to the state legislature. Formerly a member of the city board of health, the Orlando Realty Board, and a prominent civic leader, she earned the right to represent Orange County in the state house of representatives with an 800-vote margin of victory over her male opponent. Perhaps even more significantly, Ruth Bryan Owen, who later became the first American woman to serve the United States as a minister to a foreign country (Denmark in 1933), was chosen as the first female member of the United States House of Representatives from Florida and the South. Owen was elected over the longtime male incumbent in the Fourth District that stretched along the state's eastern seaboard. The daughter of Democratic party leader William Jennings Bryan, she also became a close friend of First Lady Eleanor Roosevelt.[118]

With gender bias against women beginning to fall on many levels by the late 1920s, it had become only the multiple question of person, place, and time before a woman was elected as a circuit clerk. That recognition also came in 1928. The first step was taken in June, when Doris Short Weeks of Moore Haven, seat of government for the southern county of Glades, was nominated for circuit clerk in the same primary as Greene, Fuller, and Owen. When she easily won the general election in November, she grasped the honor of first elected woman clerk. Weeks thereafter held the office continually until 1955, when she died. Her successor was another woman, Florence S. Scott.[119]

Today, memories of Doris Short Weeks and her service to Glades County remain vivid. Circuit clerk Jerry Beck well remembers Mrs. Weeks from his own boyhood and easily speaks of the high opinion in which she was held.[120] Vance Whidden, lifelong resident of Moore Haven and veteran member of the Glades County board of commissioners, stresses, in addition to Mrs. Weeks' hard work and honesty, the relationship of her friendly personality to her longevity in office. She always greeted newcomers to the courthouse with the statement, "Well, I just been wondering why you haven't been in before." According to Whidden, who had reached the age of seventy-seven when interviewed in 1996, "She met people real good." He added, "She would go beyond the call of her office to help somebody."[121]

Even though Doris Short Weeks served as Florida's first elected woman circuit clerk, another individual beat her by a few days to the honor of first woman clerk. The occurrence stemmed from the death late in 1928 of Holmes County clerk R. W. Creel. Given that Mrs. Weeks already had broken the gender barrier in November, Governor John A. Martin turned to Creel's widow, Cassie Paul Creel, as the deceased officer's successor. Mrs. Creel filled the post at the courthouse in Bonifay until her own successor was commissioned in 1933.[122]

By the time future Orange County clerk Fran Carlton was elected to the state house of representatives in 1976, she was not breaking new ground for women as had Weeks and Creel. Nor did she, after twelve years in the legislature, set a statewide precedent when she won election as circuit clerk in 1988. On the other hand, her victory was unusual in that she defeated her partisan opponent in an open contest (brought about by the incumbent's retirement) in a county where her party's voters constituted a minority. Additionally, Carlton's accomplishment was realized in the face of real public scrutiny of the contest. Orange had become a charter county in which the clerkship was one of only three of the constitutional offices that did not become a charter office.

Carlton's journey to the clerkship had been a roundabout one. Introduced to politics as a young girl when her Dixie County state representative took her to visit the legislature in 1953, she later became personally involved in politics through her interest in physical conditioning. She had started a physical fitness television program while teaching at Stetson College, as a result of which Governor Reuben Askew appointed her to a state task force to set up for Florida something comparable to President John F. Kennedy's national fitness program. When her lobbying efforts for an act accomplishing the goal met with frustration, she entered politics. Carlton won a seat in the state house and, subsequently, witnessed her ideas take the form of law, for which she offers great credit to her colleague Representative Elaine Gordon of Dade County.

As clerk, Carlton presides over a modern, technological operation in a heavily populated, complex, and growing county, and her office faces the constant and inevitable risk of becoming impersonal to the people. Asked to describe what she considers her main function, she answered: "I really think my biggest overall job is to humanize the courts for the public and provide a way for the public to interact with the courts. I find it true that our job here is to assist, to help, and to accommodate the people." She is mindful of the irony that, even though she and her staff touch the lives of every county resident, "Ours is not a very high profile job."

Carlton's dilemma is continuing to provide good service in an ever-expanding county where, as in the rest of the nation, "down-sizing" rules as the prevailing concept. Since population increases will not be matched by staff increases, her answer is to address changes through technology, while striving to avoid the problem of an impersonal, hydra-headed monster of machines that profoundly reduces the quality of human relations. Here is where elected clerks such as Carlton can provide workable answers through sensitivity to human concerns as understood through her own contact with ordinary people, whether voters or patrons of her office. Sometimes her special viewpoint as a woman also permits new insight and helps adjust priorities to address modern problems. In doing so, technological alternatives are vital (a voice response system concerning child support matters, for example, has revolutionized that aspect of the clerk's responsibilities in Orange County). Such adaptations based in technological advances, but carefully kept under human control and tempered by human concerns, give immeasurable assistance and service in areas formerly neglected.[123]

Without question women have conferred upon Florida's residents invaluable benefits through their services as clerks, but another important segment of the state's population has contributed as well and deserves recognition before this chapter closes. African Americans have labored mightily over the decades to overcome negative aspects of Florida's by-gone days in order to make their influence and talents felt in public office. The bars they encountered have been great. While blacks served in public office in substantial numbers during and after the Reconstruction era of the nineteenth century (including in the office of circuit clerk), legal proscription of the race by means of the poll tax, direct "white" primary, and other devices was firmly in place by the early twentieth century.[124]

In the circumstances, the election of Nicholas Thomas as Gadsden County circuit clerk in 1988 marked the first time in the modern era that an African American had won the post. A native of the north Florida county,

Thomas graduated from the University of Florida in 1987 with an education degree. He then returned home to teach. He was continuing his education on a master's degree when he sensed that the moment was right to run for circuit clerk. At a time when county politics had polarized around a local issue related to county services, he attracted white and black votes in order to defeat the incumbent by thirty-nine votes in a runoff election. In 1992 Thomas was reelected by over 500 votes. The victories comprise a major statement of changing times and changing attitudes. "People thought my time had come," Thomas offered as a partial explanation that gave himself too little credit.

Once in office, Thomas experienced the problems that accompany any new job, added to which were the special ones of public service that are a regular part of any circuit clerk's life. Like other clerks before him, Thomas quickly realized the enormity of the responsibilities that he had undertaken and he discovered the essential truth of what had been his own inclination, the necessity of being fair to everybody. When his pioneering efforts provoked sensitivities on some residents' parts, he stressed moderation and understanding. "I tried to downplay race," he noted. And, he was successful.

Other surprises abounded for the young man. He found the clerk's position, for instance, to be more demanding that he had anticipated. "I didn't know the personal liability," he remarked. According to Thomas, "You're responsible for everything, and you can't plead ignorance." The clerk took his work seriously: "I think being a public official is a special thing. I've wanted to be in politics since I was seven years old. I enjoy my job and what I do. Politics can be rough. If you really want to, do it. I like dealing with the public, but the public can be demanding." Thomas concluded with an important thought, though not one likely to be of concern to him soon. He declared, "Be prepared to move on if you're rejected."[125]

As these brief looks at some of Florida's circuit clerks show, laws and traditions are important to the way government operates but they are not everything. Essential to good government are talented and sensitive human beings concerned with providing the best service that the law mandates and for which taxpayers pay. Their personal experiences, temperaments, and viewpoints often make the critical difference. And, the fact that clerks hold elective office reinforces the potential for such critical human involvement, as the electoral process selects out those who evidence these very desirable traits and then holds them accountable in the tests of day to day administration.

Chapter 9

Strength Through Unity

In the post-World War II years, rapid changes in Florida brought with them a reexamination of state and county government. Was it efficient? Was there a better way to serve the needs of a state whose growth had exploded? Beyond that, few denied that the old constitution of 1885 was outmoded and needed revising or replacing. A number of people questioned whether there was a need to abandon the traditional system of having constitutional officers--the sheriff, tax collector, property appraiser, supervisor of elections, and circuit clerk--answering to the people through popular elections every four years and serving as checks and balances.

Circuit clerks came under particular fire because their many-faceted duties overlapped with those of other agencies. Modern times, critics claimed, called for cohesive administrative management, rather than a dispersal of authority.

Other concerns also confronted the clerks. As previously discussed, the idea of charter county government became current and attracted numerous supporters. It would take various forms of implementation but not of substance. Fundamentally, under charter government a popularly elected county board would, with its appointed county administrator, be the sole executive and legislative branch. Stripped of their executive authority regarding the county commission, on the one hand, clerks faced, on the other, constitutional revisionism eliminating their historic relationship with circuit judges. In seeking a more-effective judiciary, many judges wanted to have complete authority over the administration of their courts. To that end, the jurists wished to control the appointment of those who performed the duties traditionally filled by the clerks. As seen by the circuit clerks and discussed in Chapter VII, their multi-faceted historic roles faced not only revision but extinction.

The challenges resulted in cooperative action. In the interest of self-preservation and interchange of ideas and information, various circuit clerks began meeting informally and discussing the need for an organization that could foster satisfaction of mutual needs. They wanted an organization that would coordinate a program placing the clerks in touch with the legislature, as well as with each other.

The beginnings of the Florida State Association of Court Clerks, as suggested by its minutes, may be traced to 1953, but internal evidence indicates that the organization existed for some years prior to that. The Association was not formally incorporated until 1978. The 1953 meeting, held at the Seminole Hotel in Jacksonville on February 20, was called to order by President G. M. Simmons, clerk of Brevard County. Clerks from forty-six counties, plus three clerks of civil and criminal courts of record, were present. Vice President John A. Peacock of Calhoun County missed the session due to illness, but his absence was regretted--he was described as "an ardent worker" who had served the Association "for many years."[126]

Members present at the Jacksonville convention addressed a number of issues, none more important than the "fee system." In effect since 1885, and not revised since 1927, the fee system was a means of raising funds to pay salaries and expenses of clerks. The Association voted to abolish the practice and instructed its Legislative Committee to work with the legislature to effect a change.[127]

The clerks continued to meet annually and sometimes more often, but they still did not constitute a unified force. Even so, under the presidency of A. W. Nichols of Putnam County the Association adopted a new constitution in November 1958, and tangible progress was made the next year under the administration of President Francis "Cowboy" Williams of Citrus

County. By August 30, 1966, when the clerks gathered at the Everglades Hotel in Miami, S. Morgan Slaughter, clerk of Duval County, and his fellow clerks and their guests had developed an esprit that was self-perpetuating and, with the passage of time and the capricious nature of the electorate, always changing. Besides president Slaughter, numerous other clerks offered assistance to and direction for the Association. Polk County's clerk E. D. "Bud" Dixon, for example, continued as a leader among his peers. Assisting were numerous additional individuals, including V. Y. "Buck" Smith of Volusia County, James C. Watkins of Lake County, Philip A. Anderson of Walton County, Sal Geraci of Lee County, Jerry A. Scarborough of Suwannee County, and Mary B. Childs of Columbia County (who became the organization's first woman president in 1983-1984). Additionally, Gulf County's George Y. Core loaned his support.[128]

In addition to annual meetings, the clerks began to convene during the 1960s and 1970s for other gatherings and special sessions of the board of directors. The Association's members enjoyed the social aspects of these early sessions, but from the first they were serious about their purpose. For example, the Constitution Revision Committee labored diligently in 1967, at a time when Florida's government was beginning to undergo substantive reorganization. Three years afterward and after intense consideration, the Association formally acted to make its weight further felt regarding constitutional revision. In that instance it initially voted formal opposition to the proposed Judicial Article revision to the state constitution. Later, the members approved the final version.[129]

In time the Association's activities became more formalized and well established. By 1969 Barbara Nettles had become in effect what she later became in title, secretary to the Association. In future years she helped to provide order and continuity to an organization that had a yearly rotation of presidents. "Cowboy" Williams played an early and significant role as legislative consultant until bad health forced his retirement. In 1968 Charles Tom Henderson, after a period of service as an assistant attorney general for the state, commenced his tenure as the Association's counsel and contact man with the legislature, a badly needed position. Later, Fred W. Baggett succeeded Henderson. Baggett became the Association's longtime legal advisor and a vital conduit between the clerks and the lawmakers.[130]

The Association's facilities and resources expanded to meet needs brought about by Florida's population growth. At first, the Association rented rooms in Tallahassee during legislative sessions, eventually benefiting, as mentioned, from the professional contributions of Barbara Nettles, Charles Tom Henderson, and Fred W. Baggett. Then there were various physical moves of Association personnel and property in Tallahassee. Each change of address required larger administrative quarters. In any year the Association president had so many responsibilities that no amount of hard work by him could be passed along to the clerks to give them a sense of real participation in decision making. They necessarily felt left out and could only react to laws enacted at the legislative level. The clerks realized that, less and less, were they independent agents, existing in isolated little worlds known as counties, where each clerk operated uninfluenced by outside events. What happened in Tallahassee's corridors of power affected them individually, and they needed to come together in order to present their case effectively. They noticed that the perfect vehicle to bring the desired coalescence was their state Association, significant before, but more important as a bonding and social force. The body could now be used to unify the clerks in a more meaningful way, and, while becoming their voice in statewide issues, still be their instrument of service. The clerks themselves would dominate the Association and use it for their mutual interests. They would remain as separate entities, controlling the Association and letting it speak for them. The old concept of strength in unity took on a new meaning for Florida's clerks.

Early in 1990, Association president Harold Bazzel appointed Hillsborough County's clerk Richard Ake to act as the facilitator for a group of about fifteen clerks who met at Aster on the St. Johns river to work out the details. The gathering met at a fishcamp and was hosted by past Association president Ray Winstead of Brevard County. Attending were longtime Association stalwarts, as well as younger clerks. Association secretary Barbara Nettles and legislative liaison man Fred W. Baggett were also present. They convened on the weekend, taking few breaks, and hammering out the details of their as yet undefined goals. Those present would remember later that it was the older clerks who insisted on the necessity for philosophical and practical changes, and that they convinced the younger members. With Ake serving as spokesman, the group's plan was presented at Tampa in June to the Association's annual meeting. As presented, the "Mission Statement" was a concise, no-nonsense document. Its Organizational Improvements section called for employing a full-time executive director, designing a clearinghouse for legal information, and including an automated statewide net work of communication and database.[131]

The new system achieved implementation, though not without problems. A fourteen-member panel (the Association officers and board of directors) met in Tallahassee on November 13-14, 1990, to select an executive director. Hillsborough County's clerk Richard Ake chaired the session. Decorum was maintained, but there was no lack of candidly stated opinions. As a result, a few clerks withdrew from the Association, some of whom rejoined at later dates. Three candidates for executive director appeared before the committee, stated their qualifications, and responded to questions. In the end, Roger Alderman was hired by a large majority. A native of South Georgia and an experienced administrator with a master's degree in political science and economics, Alderman had served as a city and county manager in Virginia, South Carolina, and Florida. He also had held other administrative positions in Georgia. He began work on January 1, 1991.[132]

As the twenty-first century approached, Executive Director Alderman and his professional staff occupied a well-equipped building in Tallahassee and oversaw and directed the Association's expanding activities. The Association had modernized its constitution so that it now had a president and four other offices; a fifteen-member board of directors; and various standing committees and their subcommittees, as well as special committees. The Association holds its annual conference in June and has four quarterly statewide seminars. The January seminar is devoted to courts and records; the April session to finance; the September seminar to management and administration; and the one in November to technology. The Associations holds regional workshops based on need. Between February and early March, the seven-district Association convenes regional caucuses that are administrative gatherings. Meanwhile, as the Association serves its functions as coordinator and cumulative voice, the individual clerks work to maintain their historic role as constitutional officers, popularly elected to serve the people as watchdogs of government.[133]

ENDNOTES

[1] George E. Buker, "The Americanization of St. Augustine 1821-1865," p. 151, in Jean Parker Waterbury, ed., *The Oldest City: St. Augustine, Saga of Survival* (St. Augustine, 1983).

[2] *Laws of Territorial Florida* (1822), xv.

[3] Pensacola *Floridian*, October 8, 1821; Herbert J. Doherty, Jr., "Andrew Jackson's Cronies in Florida Territorial Politics, With Three Unpublished Letters to His Cronies," *Florida Historical Quarterly* 34 (July 1955), 22.

[4] Clarence E. Carter, ed., *Territorial Papers of the United States* vols. XXII-XXVI, *Florida Territory* (Washington, D.C., 1956-1962), XXII, 284 (hereinafter, *TP*).

[5] John Spencer Bassett, comp., *Correspondence of Andrew Jackson*, 6 vols. (Washington, D.C., 1926-1935), III, 129.

[6] *Laws of Territorial Florida* (1824), 247-51.

[7] James M. Denham, "From a Territorial to a State Judiciary: Florida's Antebellum Courts and Judges," *Florida Historical Quarterly* 73 (April 1995), 445.

[8] St. Augustine *Florida Herald*, May 5, 1830, quoted in Denham, "From a Territorial to a State Judiciary," 445.

[9] E. A. Ware to N. P. Bemis, July 27, 1846, State Comptroller's Correspondence, Record Group 350, Series 554, box 1, folder 2, Florida State Archives, Tallahassee.

[10] *Laws of Territorial Florida* (1822), xx.

[11] *TP*, XXIII, 66-67.

[12] Ibid., 1027-28.

[13] *Laws of Territorial Florida* (1822), 4.

[14] Ibid., (1823), 9.

[15] Ibid., 106-07.

[16] Ibid., (1824), 279.

[17] Ibid., (1828), 209-12.

[18] Ibid.

[19] Ibid., 172-73.

[20] Ibid., (1829), 46-47.

[21] Ibid., (1833), 42-49.

[22] Elizabeth H. Sims, *A History of Madison County, Florida* (Madison: Madison County Historical Society, 1986), 28.

[23] *Laws of Territorial Florida* (1844), 37-38.

[24] Canter Brown, Jr., "Race Relations in Territorial Florida, 1821-1845," *Florida Historical Quarterly* 73 (January 1995), 287-304.

[25] Dorothy Dodd, *Florida Becomes a State* (Tallahassee: Florida Centennial Commission, 1945), 37-46.

[26] Ibid., 47-66. Dodd's book contains an introduction by William T. Cash, her overview, and a series of documents supplied by her, including *The Journal of the Proceedings of a Convention of Delegates To Form a Constitution for the People of Florida, Held at St. Joseph, December, 1838* (St. Joseph: Times Office, 1839). This document will be cited hereafter as *Convention Proceedings 1838-1839*.

[27] Dodd, *Florida Becomes a State*, 52.

[28] *Convention Proceedings 1838-1839*, 164.

[29] Dodd, *Florida Becomes a State*, 52.

[30] *Convention Proceedings 1838-1839*, 198.

[31] Dodd, *Florida Becomes a State*, 314.

[32] *Convention Proceedings 1838-1839*, 207-08.

[33] Dodd, *Florida Becomes a State*, 69.

[34] Ibid., 69-70.

[35] On the rise of Florida's political parties and the fight over statehood, see Herbert J. Doherty, *The Whigs of Florida 1845-1854* (Gainesville: University Press of Florida, 1959); idem., *Richard Keith Call, Southern Unionist* (Gainesville: University Press of Florida, 1961), 108-34; and Canter Brown, Jr., "Ossian Bingley Hart, Florida's Loyalist Reconstruction Governor" (Ph.D. dissertation, Florida State University, 1994), 68-73, 107-23.

[36] See Canter Brown, Jr., *Florida Peace River Frontier* (Orlando: University of Central Florida Press, 1991).

[37] Hampton Dunn, *Back Home, A History of Citrus County, Florida* (Clearwater: Citrus County Bicentennial Committee, 1975), 100-02.

[38] Sims, *History of Madison County*, 28-29.

[39] Eloise Robinson and Louis Hickman Chazal, *Ocali Country Kingdom of the Sun, A History of Marion County, Florida* (Ocala: Marion Publishing Company, 1968), 41-49.

[40] Mary Oakley McRory and Edith Clark Barrows, *History of Jefferson County, Florida* (Monticello: Kiwanis Club, 1935), 17.

[41] Ibid., 18-19; Jerrell H. Shofner, *History of Jefferson County* (Tallahassee: Sentry Press, 1976), 458-59.

[42] Oration of John F. Bartholf, Pine Level, Florida, July 4, 1876, U. S. Centennial Orations 1876, Library of Congress, Washington, DC.

[43] Tampa *Florida Peninsular*, January 12, 1870.

[44] Lillie B. McDuffie, *The Lures of Manatee* (Bradenton: Manatee County Historical Society, 1961), 111.

[45] M. F. Hetherington, *History of Polk County, Florida, Narrative and Biographical* (St. Augustine: Record Company, 1928), 39.

[46] *Who's Who Politically Speaking in Clay County, Florida 1856-1986* (Green Cove Springs: Clay County Board of Commissioners, 1986), 5.

[47] Jacksonville *News*, November 13, 1846; Edward F. Keuchel, *A History of Columbia County, Florida* (Tallahassee: Sentry Press, 1981), 128-29.

[48] Marianna *Florida Whig*, December 2, 1848.

[49] Tallahassee *Floridian & Journal*, November 17, 1849.

[50] Entry of September 21, 1860, Washington Mackey Ives diary, 1860-1862, M88-45, Florida State Archives, Tallahassee.

[51] Eve Bacon, *Orlando: A Centennial History*, 2 vols. (Chuluota: Mickler House Publishers, 1975), I, 1-3, 14.

[52] Fritz W. Bucholz, *History of Alachua County, Florida, Narrative and Biography* (St. Augustine: The Record Company, 1929), 61-63, 157-58.

[53] McDuffie, *Lures of Manatee*, 102, 108-11.

[54] James Johnson to Florida comptroller, c. 1857, copy in collection of Dr. James M. Denham, Florida Southern College, Lakeland.

[55] *Laws of Territorial Florida* (1832), 96-97.

[56] St. Augustine *News*, August 2, 1845.

[57] *Laws of Florida* (1845), 8.

[58] Ibid., 10.

[59] Ibid.

[60] Returns of elections held in Columbia County, October 6, 1845, Election Returns, record group 156, series 21, box 6, FSA; Lake City *Florida Index*, January 11, 1901; *Roster of State and County Officers Commissioned by the Governor of Florida 1845-1868* (Jacksonville: Florida Historical Records Survey, 1941), 66.

[61] Denham, "From a Territorial to a State Judiciary," 455.

[62] *Roster of State and County Officers*; John Hood Baxley, Julius J. Gordon, and Diane Moore Rodriguez, *Oaklawn Cemetery and St. Louis Catholic Cemetery: Biographical & Historical Gleanings*, 2 vols. (Tampa: Baxley, Gordon & Rodriguez, 1991), 178.

[63] *Roster of State and County Officials*; Brown, "Ossian Bingley Hart," 117-18, 447; *Weekly Tallahasseean*, February 20, 1903; Lake City *Florida Index*, February 20, 1903.

[64] On the Third Seminole War, see James W. Covington, *The Billy Bowlegs War, 1855-1858: The Final Stand of the Seminoles Against the Whites* (Chuluota: Mickler House Publishers, 1982).

[65] On Civil War era Florida, see John E. Johns, *Florida During the Civil War* (Gainesville: University of Florida Press, 1963); and Canter Brown, Jr., "The Civil War, 1861-1865" in Michael V. Gannon, ed., *The New History of Florida* (Gainesville: University Presses of Florida, 1996), 231-48.

[66] LeRoy Collins, *Forerunners Courageous, Stories of Frontier Florida* (Tallahassee: Colcade Publishers, 1971), 155.

[67] David W. Hartman and David Coles, *Biographical Rosters of Florida's Confederate and Union Soldiers 1861-1865*, 6 vols. (Wilmington, NC: Broadfoot Publishing Co., 1995), II, 484, 725-26.

[68]Jefferson B. Browne, *Key West, The Old and The New* (St. Augustine: The Record Co., 1912; reprint ed., Gainesville: University of Florida Press, 1973), 93, 211; Hartman and Coles, *Biographical Rosters*, II, 772.

[69]E. Merton Coulter, *The Confederate States of America 1861-1865* (Baton Rouge: Louisiana State University Press, 1950), 315.

[70]T. Frederick Davis, *History of Jacksonville, Florida and Vicinity, 1513 to 1924* (Jacksonville: Florida Historical Society, 1925; reprint ed., Jacksonville: San Marco Bookstore, 1990), 117; O. B. Hart to F. F. L'Engle, September 22, 1863, in Dena E. Snodgrass Collection, P. K. Yonge Library of Florida History, University of Florida, Gainesville.

[71]Samuel Proctor, ed., *Florida A Hundred Years Ago* (Coral Gables: Florida Library and Historical Commission and Civil War Centennial Committee, 1961-1965), January 1965, n.p.

[72]Billie Ford Snider and Janice B. Palmer, *Spanish Plat Book of Land Records of the District of Pensacola, Province of West Florida, British and Spanish Land Grants 1763-1821* (Pensacola: Antique Compiling, 1994), 3-4; Receipt of J. H. Alexander, July 3, 1865, collection of Historic Pensacola Preservation Board.

[73]Unsigned letter, dated Greenville, Alabama, June 16, 1864, collection of Historical Pensacola Preservation Board.

[74]Holmes Melton, Jr., *Lafayette County History and Heritage* (Mayo: Holmes M. Melton, Jr., 1974), 71.

[75]Grace Emerick Moses, *Footprints Along the Suwannee* (Branford: Grace Emerick Moses, 1981), 12.

[76]Catharine S. Hart to "My dear Mother, Sisters & Brothers," January 5, 1865, Snodgrass Collection.

[77]On the post-Civil War era in Florida, see Jerrell H. Shofner, *Nor Is It Over Yet: Florida in the Era of Reconstruction, 1863-1877* (Gainesville: University of Florida Press, 1974); and Canter Brown, Jr., "Ossian Bingley Hart."

[78]Shofner, *Nor Is It Over Yet*, 43; Browne, *Key West*, 90-93, 211, 219; Hartman and Coles, *Biographical Rosters*, II, 772.

[79]Brown, *Florida's Peace River Frontier*, 186-87.

[80]See Eric Foner, *Reconstruction: America's Unfinished Revolution, 1863-1877* (New York: Harper & Row, 1988).

[81]Shofner, *Nor Is It Over Yet*, 157-85; Brown, "Ossian Bingley Hart," 327-50.

[82]John Wallace, *Carpetbag Rule in Florida: The Inside Workings of the Reconstruction of Civil Government in Florida After the Close of the Civil War* (Jacksonville: Da Costa Printing and Publishing House, 1888; reprint ed., Kennesaw, GA: Continental Book Company, 1959), 419.

[83]*Laws of Florida* (1868), 2-8, 17-21, 25-28, 92, 107-11, 163.

[84]Canter Brown, Jr., "'Where are now the hopes I cherished?' The Life and Times of Robert Meacham," *Florida Historical Quarterly* 69 (July 1990), 1-12; Jacksonville *Florida Union*, December 5, 1868.

[85] Jefferson County Circuit Court Records, Order Book B, 495; Shofner, *Jefferson County*, 314-15.

[86] Canter Brown, Jr., *Florida's Black Public Officials, 1867-1924* (publication in press), n.p.

[87] Jerrell H. Shofner, *Jackson County, Florida--A History* (Marianna: Jackson County Heritage Association, 1985), 280.

[88] Canter Brown, Jr., *Florida's Peace River Frontier*, 210-13.

[89] Tallahassee *Sentinel*, quoted in Jacksonville *Florida Union*, January 15, 1877.

[90] Brown, *Florida's Peace River Frontier*, 293.

[91] Tampa *Sunland Tribune*, June 12, 1879; Tampa *Guardian*, December 6, 13, 1879.

[92] Jacksonville *Weekly Florida Union*, July 14, 1877; Tallahassee *Weekly Floridian*, June 24, 1877.

[93] Tampa *Sunland Tribune*, October 6, 13, November 10, 1877.

[94] On Redemption-era politics, generally, see Edward C. Williamson, *Florida Politics During the Gilded Age* (Gainesville: University of Florida Press, 1976).

[95] Edward C. Williamson, "The Constitutional Convention of 1885," *Florida Historical Quarterly* 41 (October 1962), 121-22.

[96] New York *Freeman*, September 12, 1885.

[97] *Journal of the Proceedings of the Constitutional Convention of the State of Florida, Which Convened at the Capitol at Tallahassee on Tuesday, June 9, 1885* (Tallahassee: N. M. Bowden, State Printer, 1885), 470.

[98] Brown, *Florida's Black Public Officials*, n.p.

[99] Gannon, *New History of Florida*, 267-78.

[100] Larry Berkson and Steven Hays, "The Forgotten Politicians: Court Clerks," *University of Miami Law Review* 30 (Spring 1976), 499-516.

[101] Ibid.

[102] For an informed discussion, see Raymond A. Mohl and Gary R. Mormino, "The Big Change in the Sunshine State: A Social History of Modern Florida," in Gannon, *New History of Florida*, at pps. 418-45.

[103] For the chart, see Maxine D. Jones, "The African-American Experience in Twentieth-Century Florida," in Gannon, *New History of Florida*, at p. 379.

[104] See Morris and Morris, *Florida Handbook 1995-1996*, 429-445.

[105] See Raymond A. Mohl and George E. Pozzetta, "From Migration to Multiculturalism: A History of Florida Immigration," in Gannon, *New History of Florida*, at pps. 391-417.

[106] See Jones, "African-American Experience," 373-90.

[107] See David R. Colburn, "Florida Politics in the Twentieth Century," in Gannon, *New History of Florida*, at pps. 344-72. See also David R. Colburn and Richard K. Scher, *Florida's Gubernatorial Politics in the Twentieth Century* (Tallahassee: Florida State University Press, 1980).

[108] Lucy Graetz, "Charter Government in Florida: Past Litigation and Future Proposals," *University of Florida Law Review* 33 (Summer 1981), 505, 508; Steven L. Sparkman, "The History and Status of Local Government Powers in Florida," *University of Florida Law Review* 35 (Winter 1973), 282-83.

[109] Graetz, "Charter County Government," 508-10; Sparkman, "History and Status of Local Government Powers," 287.

[110] Graetz, "Charter County Government," 510-12; Sparkman, "History and Status of Local Government Powers," 285-90.

[111] Talbot "Sandy" D'Alemberte, "Judicial Reform--Now or Never," *Florida Bar Journal* (February 1972), 68-71.

[112] Joseph W. Little, "An Overview of the Historical Development of the Judicial Article of the Florida Constitution," *Stetson Law Review* (Fall 1989), 28.

[113] Personal interview with Roger Alderman by William Warren Rogers, April 26, 1996.

[114] Copies of circuit and supreme court case decisions on file at Florida Association of Court Clerks and Comptrollers, Tallahassee.

[115] Tim Sanders interviews, March 28, April 22, 1996.

[116] Ernie Lee Magaha interview, February 1, 1996.

[117] Allen Morris, *Florida Handbook 1995-1996* (Tallahassee: Peninsular Publishing Co., 1996), 249-50.

[118] Ibid.; Jacksonville *Florida Times-Union*, June 9, 1928; Sarah P. Vickers, "The Life of Ruth Bryan Owen: Florida's First Congresswoman and America's First Woman Diplomat" (Ph.D. dissertation, Florida State University, 1994), chapters V-X.

[119] *Report of the Secretary of State of the State of Florida for the Period Beginning January 1, 1929, and Ending December 31, 1930* (Tallahassee: T. J. Appleyard, 1931), 88; Glades County Board of Commissioners, *Glades County, Florida, History* (Moore Haven: Rainbow Books, 1985), 52.

[120] Jerry Beck interview, February 28, 1996.

[121] Vance Whidden interview, February 28, 1996.

[122] *Report of the Secretary of State of the State of Florida for the Period Beginning January 1, 1927, and Ending December 31, 1928* (Marianna: Fla. Ind. School for Boys, 1929), 115; records of commissions, Record Group 156, Series 259, Florida State Archives.

[123] Fran Carlton interview, April 16, 1996.

[124] Gannon, *New History of Florida*, 373-89.

[125] Nicholas Thomas interview, February 22, 1996.

[126] Minutes of the Florida Association of Court Clerks and Comptrollers, vol. I, February 20, 1953 (hereinafter cited as Minutes).

[127] Ibid.

[128] Ibid., entries of 1954-1984.

[129] Ibid., II, 1967, June 1970.

[130] Personal interview, Barbara Nettles by the authors, April 6, 1996; Minutes, II, August 30, 1966.

[131] Barbara Nettles interview; Personal interview, Fred W. Baggett by William Warren Rogers, June 5, 1996. "Florida Association of Court Clerks Mission Statement" on file at the Florida Association of Court Clerks and Comptrollers, Tallahassee.

[132] Personal interview, Roger Alderman by William Warren Rogers, April 26, 1996; Minutes, III, November 13-14, 1990.

[133] Roger Alderman interview.

BIBLIOGRAPHY

Manuscripts

Denham, James M. Historical notes and files. Lakeland.
Florida Association of Court Clerks and Comptrollers. Minutes. Tallahassee, Florida.

Historic Pensacola Preservation Board. Historical collection.
Ives, Washington Mackey. Diary, 1860-1862. M88-45, Florida State Archives.

Snodgrass, Dena E. Collection. P. K. Yonge Library of Florida History, University of Florida, Gainesville.

U. S. Centennial Orations, 1876. Library of Congress. V.

Interviews

[All interviews conducted by the authors; notes in the collections of the authors]

Alderman, Roger. Personal interview, April 26, 1996.

Baggett, Fred W. Personal interview at Tallahassee, June 5, 1996.

Beck, Jerry. Telephone interview, February 28, 1996.

Carlton, Fran. Telephone interview, April 16, 1996.

Magaha, Ernie Lee. Personal interview at Sandestin, February 1, 1996.

Nettles, Barbara. Personal interview at headquarters of the Florida Association of Court Clerks and Comptrollers, Tallahassee, April 6, 1996.

Sanders, Tim. Personal interview at Madison County Courthouse, Madison, March 28, 1996, and telephone interview, April 22, 1996.

Thomas, Nicholas. Personal interview at Gadsden County Courthouse, Quincy, February 22, 1996.

Whidden, Vance. Telephone interview, February 28, 1996.

Public Documents and Public Records

Carter, Clarence E., ed. *Territorial Papers of the United States*, vols. XXII-XXVI, *Florida Territory*. Washington, DC: US Government Printing Office, 1956-1962.

Florida. *Journal of the Proceedings of a Convention of Delegates To Form a Constitution for the People of Florida, Held at St. Joseph, December, 1838.* St. Joseph: times Office, 1839.

_____. *Journal of the Proceedings of the Constitutional Convention of the State of Florida, Which Convened at the Capitol at Tallahassee on Tuesday, June 9, 1885.* Tallahassee: N. M. Bowden, State Printer, 1885.

_____. *Laws of Florida*, 1845-1996.

_____. *Laws of Territorial Florida*, 1822-1845.

_____. *Report of the Secretay of State of the State of Florida for the Period Beginning January 1, 1927, and Ending December 31, 1928.* Marianna: Fla. Ind. School for Boys, 1929.

_____. *Report of the Secretary of State of the State of Florida for the Period Beginning January 1, 1929, and Ending December 31, 1930.* Tallahassee: T. J. Appleyard, 1931.

Florida State Archives. Commissions, 1827-1978. Record Group 156, Series 259.

_____. Election Returns. Record Group 156, Series 21.

_____. State Comptroller's Correspondence. Record Group 350, Series 554.

Jefferson County. Circuit Court Records. Jefferson County Courthouse, Monticello.

Roster of State and County Officers Commissioned by the Governor of Florida 1845-1868. Jacksonville: Florida Historical Records Survey, 1941.

Newspapers

Jacksonville *Florida Times-Union*, 1928.
Jacksonville *Florida Union*, 1868-1877.
Jacksonville *News*, 1846.
Jacksonville *Weekly Florida Union*, 1877.
Lake City *Florida Index*, 1901-1903.
Marianna *Whig*, 1848.
New York *Freeman*, 1885.
Pensacola *Floridian*, 1821.
St. Augustine *Florida Herald*, 1830.
St. Augustine *News*, 1845.
Tallahassee *Floridian & Journal*, 1849.
Tallahassee *Sentinel*, 1877.
Tallahassee *Weekly Floridian*, 1877.
Tampa *Florida Peninsular*, 1870.
Tampa *Guardian*, 1879.
Tampa *Sunland Tribune*, 1877-1879.
Weekly Tallahassean, 1903.

Secondary Sources

Bacon, Eve. *Orlando: A Centennial History*. 2 vols. Chuluota: Mickler House Publishers, 1975.

Bassett, John Spencer, comp. *Correspondence of Andrew Jackson*. 6 vols. Washington, DC: Carnegie Institution of Washington, 1926-1935.

Baxley, John Hood, Julius J. Gordon, and Diane Moore Rodriguez. *Oaklawn Cemetery and St. Louis Catholic Cemetery: Biographical & Historical Gleanings*. 2 vols. Tampa: Baxley, gordon & Rodriguez, 1991.

Berkson, Larry, and Steven Hays. "The Forgotten Politicians: Court Clerks." *University of Miami Law Review* 30 (Spring 1976): 499-516.

Brown, Canter, Jr. *Florida's Peace River Frontier*. Orlando: University of Central Florida Press, 1991.

_____. "Ossian Bingley Hart, Florida's Loyalist Reconstruction Governor." Ph.D. dissertation, Florida State University, 1994.

_____. "Race Relations in Territorial Florida, 1821-1845." *Florida Historical Quarterly* 73 (January 1995): 287-307.

_____. "'Where are now the hopes I cherished?' The Life and Times of Robert Meacham." *Florida Historical Quarterly* 69 (July 1990): 1-36.

Browne, Jefferson B. *Key West, The Old and The New*. St. Augustine: The Record Company, 1912. Reprint ed., Gainesville: University of Florida Press, 1973.

Bucholz, Fritz W. *History of Alachua County, Florida, Narrative and Biography*. St. Augustine: The Record Company, 1929.

Buker, George E. "The Americanization of St. Augustine 1821-1865." In *The Oldest City: St. Augustine, Saga of Survival*. Edited by Jean Parker Waterbury. St. Augustine: St. Augustine Historical Society, 1983.

Colburn, David R., and Richard K. Scher. *Florida's Gubernatorial Politics in the Twentieth Century*. Tallahassee: Florida State University Press, 1980.

Collins, LeRoy. *Forerunners Courageous, Stories of Frontier Florida*. Tallahassee: Colcade Publishers, 1971.

Coulter, E. Merton. *The Confederate States of America 1861-1865*. Baton Rouge: Louisiana State University Press, 1950.

Covington, James W. *The Billy Bowlegs War, 1855-1858: The Final Stand of the Seminoles Against the Whites*. Chuluota: Mickler House Publishers, 1982.

D'Alemberte, Talbot "Sandy." "Judicial Reform--Now or Never." *Florida Bar Journal* (February 1972): 68-71.

Davis, T. Frederick. *History of Jacksonville, Florida and Vicinity, 1513 to 1924.* Jacksonville: Florida Historical Society, 1925. Reprinted., Jacksonville: San Marco Bookstore, 1990.

Denham, James M. "From a Territorial to a State Judiciary: Florida's Antebellum Courts and Judges." *Florida Historical Quarterly* 73 (April 1995): 443-55.

Dodd, Dorothy. *Florida Becomes a State.* Tallahassee: Florida Centennial Commission, 1945.

Doherty, Herbert J. "Andrew Jackson's Cronies in Florida Territorial Politics, With Three Unpublished Letters to His Cronies." *Florida Historical Quarterly* 34 (July 1955): 3-29.

_____. *Richard Keith Call: Southern Unionist.* Gainesville: University Press of Florida, 1961.

_____. *The Whigs of Florida 1845-1854.* Gainesville: University Press of Florida, 1959.

Dunn, Hampton. *Back Home, A History of Citrus County, Florida.* Clearwater: Citrus County Bicentennial Committee, 1975.

Foner, Eric. *Reconstruction: America's Unfinished Revolution, 1863-1877.* New York: Harper & Row, 1988.

Gannon, Michael V., ed. *The New History of Florida.* Gainesville: University Presses of Florida, 1996.

Glades County, Board of Commissioners. *Glades County, Florida, History.* Moore Haven: Rainbow Books, 1985.

Graetz, Lucy. "Charter Government in Florida: Past Litigation and Future Proposals." *University of Florida Law Review* 33 (Summer 1981): 505-38.

Hartman, David W., and David Coles. *Biographical Rosters of Florida's Confederate and Union Soldiers 1861-1865.* 6 vols. Wilmington, NC: Broadfoot Publishing Co., 1995.

Hetherington, M. F. *History of Polk County, Florida, Narrative and Biographical.* St. Augustine: Record Company, 1928.

Johns, John E. *Florida During the Civil War*. Gainesville: University of Florida Press, 1963.

Keuchel, Edward F. *A History of Columbia County, Florida*. Tallahassee: Sentry Press, 1981.

Little, Joseph W. "An Overview of the Historical Development of the Judicial Article of the Florida Constitution." *Stetson Law Review* (Fall 1989): 1-42.

McDuffie, Lillie B. *The Lures of Manatee*. Bradenton: Manatee County History Society, 1961.

McRory, Mary Oakley, and Edith Clark Barrows. *History of Jefferson County, Florida*. Monticello: Kiwanis Club, 1935.

Melton, Holmes, Jr. *Lafayette County History and Heritage*. Mayo: Holmes M. Melton, Jr., 1974.

Moore-Wilson, Minnie. *History of Osceola County Florida Frontier Life*. Orlando: Inland Press, 1935.

Morris, Allen. *The Florida Handbook 1995-1996*. Tallahassee: Peninsular Publishing Co., 1996.

Moses, Grace Emerick. *Footprints Along the Suwannee*. Branford: Grace Emerick Moses, 1981.

Proctor, Samuel, ed. *Florida A Hundred Years Ago*. Coral Gables: Florida Library and Historical Commission and Civil War Centennial Committee, 1961-1965.

Robinson, Eloise, and Louis Hickman Chazal. *Ocali Country Kingdom of the Sun, A History of Marion County, Florida*. Ocala: Marion Publishing Company, 1968.

Shofner, Jerrell H. *History of Jefferson County*. Tallahassee: Sentry Press, 1976.

_____. *Jackson County, Florida--A History*. Marianna: Jackson County Heritage Association, 1985.

_____. *Nor Is It Over Yet: Florida in the Era of Reconstruction, 1863-1877.* Gainesville: University of Florida Press, 1974.

Sims, Elizabeth H. *A History of Madison County, Florida.* Madison: Madison County Historical Society, 1986.

Snider, Billie Ford, and Janice B. Palmer. *Spanish Plat Book of Land Records of the District of Pensacola, Province of West Florida, British and Spanish Land Grants 1763-1821.* Pensacola: Antique Compiling, 1994.

Sparkman, Steven L. "The History and Status of Local Government Powers in Florida." *University of Florida Law Review* 35 (Winter 1973): 271-307.

Vickers, Sarah P. "The Life of Ruth Bryan Owen: Florida's First Congresswoman and America's First Woman Diplomat." Ph.D. dissertation, Florida State University, 1994.

Wallace, John. *Carpetbag Rule in Florida: The Inside Workings of the Reconstruction of Civil Government in Florida After the Close of the Civil War.* Jacksonville: Da Costa Printing and Publishing House, 1888. Reprint ed., Kennesaw, GA: Continental Book Company, 1959.
Who's Who Politically Speaking in Clay County, Florida 1856-1986. Green Cove Springs: Clay County Board of Commissioners, 1986.

Williamson, Edward C. "The Constitutional Convention of 1885." *Florida Historical Quarterly* 41 (October 1862): 116-26.

_____. *Florida Politics During the Gilded Age.* Gainesville: University of Florida Press, 1976.

Index

A

Adams, John Quincy, President and Secretary of State, 10
Adams-Onis Treaty, 5
Ake, Richard, 95-96
Alabama, 6
Alachua, 37
Alachua County, 36-37, 56, 77
Alderman, Roger, 97-98
Allen, Richard C., 22
Alligator, 33
Anderson, Philip A., 94
Apalachicola River, 20
Appomattox Courthouse, Va., 52
Arcadia, 30
Askew, Reuben, 86
Auburn University, 82

B

Baggett, Fred W., 95-96
Baltzell, Thomas, 22
Bartholf, Andrew, 57
Barthoff, John Francis, 30-31
Bartholf, John F., 57
Bartow, 32
Barry, William T., 7
Bay County, 71
Bazzel, Harold, 96
Beck, Jerry, 85
Berkson, Larry, 65-67

Black Codes, 52
blacks, 6, 72-73, 88
Blount, Jehu J., 45
Bradenton, 30, 37
Breckinridge, J.C., 8
Brevard County, 93, 96
Brown decision, 72
Broward County, 71
Bryan, Council, 45
Bryan, William Jennings, 84
Bulloch, Robert, 39

C

Caldwell, B. F., 35
Calhoun County, 22, 93
Call, Richard Keith, 8, 21, 25, 45
Callahan, 46
Caribbean-Latin Americans, 72
Carlton, Fran, 86-88
Carruth, Cotesworth L., 44
Carter, Elizabeth, 28
Carter, Levi, 43-44
Castro, Fidel, 71
Charlotte County, 71
charter counties, 74-76, 86, 92
"checks and balances," vii, 4, 75
Childs, Mary B., 94
Chiles, Lawton, 75
Chipley, William D., 63
Citrus County, 28, 93-94
civil law, 2

Civil War, 1, 37-38, 45, 47-48, 51-52
Clay County, 32
Collier County, 71
Columbia County, 11, 33-34, 36, 43-44
Constitution Revision Committee, 94-95
Core, George Y., 94
Creek Indians, 6
Creel, Cassie Paul, 86
Creel, R. W., 86
Crittenden, John J., 7
Crusoe, Peter A., 45, 52
Cubans, 71

D

DaCosta, Aaron W., 46
Dade County, 74-75, 87
de la Rusa, Filo E., 46-47
Dell's, 36
Denham, James M., 12, 44
Denmark, 84
Dixie County, 71, 86
Dixon, E. D. "Bud," 94
Dodd, Dorothy, 23
Drew, George F., 57-58
Duval County, 11, 15, 46, 61, 62, 94
DuVal, William Pope, 10-11, 22, 24

E

East Florida, 6, 8-10, 20-22, 25, 28
England (Great Britain), 3
English common law, 3
Enterprise (Benson Springs), 34
Escambia County, 7, 46, 81, 82
Europe, 3

F

"fee system," 93
Fifth Florida Infantry (CSA), 45
Finlayson, Dr. John L., 57
First Seminole War, 5
Flagler County, 71
Flagler, Henry M., 63
Florida constitution of 1838-1839, 19-20, 22-25; of 1865, 52; of 1868, 53-55; of 1885, 60-62, 76; of 1968, 73, 76; judicial amendment of 1970 rejected, 76
judicial amendment of 1972, ratified, 76-77
Florida Legislative Council, 8, 13
Florida, population of, 70
Florida Railroad, 37
Florida Railroad Commission, 84
Florida State Association of Court Clerks and Comptrollers, 76, 93-98
Florida Union, 55
Florida Whig, 34
Fort Gatlin, 34
Fort King, 28-29
free blacks, 20
Fuller, Edna Giles, 84-85

G

Gadsen County, 11, 34, 88
Gadsen, James, 8
Gainesville, 37
Gambia, John C., 56
Georgia, 97
Geraci, Sal, 94
Gettis, James, 53
Gibbs, George, 7
Gibbs, Jonathan C., 61

Gibbs, Thomas V., 61
Gilchrist County, 71
Glades County, 71, 85
Glazier, Ezekiel, 38
Gordon, Elaine, 87
"government in the sunshine," 75
Great Depression, 70-71
Great Freeze of 1895, 41
Green Cove Springs, 33
Green, James D., 57-59
Greene, Mamie Eaton, 84-85
Greenville, Al., 46
Guardian, 59
Gulf County, 71, 94

H

Hammurabi, 2
Hammurabic Code, 2-3
Hankins, Dennis, 16-17
Hardee County, 71
Harmon, Henry S., 56
Harris, ?, 39
Hart, Catharine, 49
Hays, Steven, 65-67
Henderson, Charles Tom, 95
Hendry County, 71
Hernando County, 44, 59, 60-61
Higginbotham, David H., 46
Highlands County, 71
Hillsborough County, 12-13, 44, 96
Hispanic-Americans, 71
Hixtown (Hickstown), 28
Hogtown, 37
Holmes County, 86
Hughey, James, 35
Hunt, William H., 14
Hunter, Hugh G., 43

I

Independent movement, 60

Indian River County, 71
Indians, 20-21
Inverness, 28
Iowa, 25, 27

J

Jackson County, 11, 22, 34, 57-58
Jackson County War, 57
Jackson, President and Military Governor of Florida, 5-11, 13, 19, 20, 25
Jackson, Rachel, 6
Jacksonian democracy, 16-17, 19, 61
Jacksonville, 46, 55, 93
Jay, 82
Jefferson County, 18, 28-30, 32, 55-56
Jefferson, President Thomas, 6
Jernigan, Aaron, 34-35
Jim Crowism, 72
Johnson, James, 38
Johnson, President Andrew, 52
Jones, William Kinnon, 47-48

K

Keen, George G., 43
Kennedy, President John F., 87
Kentucky, 7, 10
Key West, 45, 52, 59
Knights of Labor, 62

L

Lafayette County, 47-48
Lake City, 33, 46
Lake County, 94
Lee County, 94

Lee, Edmund, 37-38
Lee, Electra, 38
Lee, General Robert E., 52
Lee, Joseph E., 62
Legislative Reorganization Act of 1969, 73
Leon County, 11, 22, 44-45
Levy [Yulee], David, 25-26, 37
Lincoln, President Abraham, 52
Louisiana, 3

M

McLeod, Alexander, 29
Madison County, 16, 20, 28, 44, 56, 80
Magaha, Ernie Lee, 81-83
Manatee County, 30-32, 37-38, 44-45, 53, 57-59
Mann, Austin S., 61
Mannfield, 28
Marianna, 20, 34, 57
Marion County, 28-29, 38
Martin County, 71
Martin, John A., 86
Martin, Thomas Zachariah, 80
Marvin, William, 52
Meacham, Robert, 55-56
Mesopotamia, 2
Methodists, 44
Mexicans, 72
Miami, 94
Middle Florida, 20-21, 25, 29, 48, 54
Military Reconstruction Acts, 53
Miller, G. D., 33
Miller, John 7-9, 13
"Mission Statement," 97
Missouri, 74
Mitchell, Henry L., 59
Mizell, Enoch E., 32
Monroe County, 11, 45, 52
Monroe, President James, 5-6, 9-10
Montesquieu, 4
Monticello, 20, 84
Moore Haven, 85
Moseley, William D., 41
Mosquito County, 17, 34
Myers, Oscar A., 44

N

Napoleonic Code, 3
Nassau County, 46
Nettles, Barbara, 95-97
New Orleans, La., 5
New Smyrna, 34
New York, 56
New York City, 31
Newnansville, 36-37
Newton, 28
Nichols, A. W., 93
Nineteenth Amendment, 84

O

Ocala, 29
Okaloosa County, 71
Okeechobee County, 71
Old Troy, 47-48
Orange County, 17, 34-35, 84, 86, 88
Orlando, 34, 84
Orlando Realty Board, 84
Owen, Ruth Bryan, 84-85

P

Palm Beach County, 71
Panic of 1837, 21
Partridge, James M., 22
Pasco, Jefferson, 55
Peacock, John A., 93
Pennsylvania, 56

Pensacola, 6-8, 13, 46-47, 82
Perdido River, 6
Perry, James Porter, 80
Perry, John, 80
Perry, Leighton Maynard, 80
Pine Level, 30-31, 38
Pinellas County, 71
Plant, Henry B., 63
Plessy v. *Ferguson,* 72
Polk County, 32-45, 94
poll tax, 62, 88
Powers, Curtis A., 77
Presbyterians, 37
Purnam, William J., 57-58
Putnam County, 93

Q

Quincy, 20-34

R

railroads, 41, 63
Randolph, John, 6
Reconstruction, 133, 37-38, 51, 53, 57-58, 62-63, 88
Reed, Harrison, 54-56
Reid, Robert Raymond, 22, 25
Robinson, John, 29
Roosevelt, Eleanor, 84
Rosewood, 72
Russia, 5

S

San Pedro, 28
Sanders, Tim, 80-81, 83
Sarasota County, 71
Scarborough, Jerry A., 94

Scarborough, Stirling, 43-44
Scott, Florence, S., 85
secession, 45
Second Seminole War, 13, 24
Seminole County, 71
Seventh Florida (CSA), 45
Simmons, G.M., 93
slavery, 20, 52
Smith, V. Y. "Buck," 94
South Carolina, 20, 80, 97
Spain, 5, 8-9
Sparkman, Stephen M., 59
Spirit of the Laws, 4
Spottswood, John G., 58-59
Spring Grove, 36
St. Augustine, 6-7, 12
St. Clair, the Rev. Arthur, 59
St. Johns County, 7, 15
St. Johns River, 96
St. Joseph, 3
Stearns, Marcellus, 57
Stetson College, 86
Summerlin, Jacob, 32, 35
Suwannee County, 94
Suwannee River, 6, 20

T

Tallahassee, 20, 41-42, 52, 61, 95-98
Tampa, 45, 49, 53, 59, 97
Tennessee, 10
Third Seminole (Billy Bowlegs) War, 44-45
Thomas, Nicholas, 88-89
Tyler, President John, 26

U

Union Bank of Florida, 21
Union County, 71

United States Constitution, 4
University of Florida, 88

V

Van Buren, President Martin, 25
Virginia, 6, 10, 97
Volusia County, 34, 94

W

Walton County, 94
Ward, George T., 22
Ware, E. A., 12-13
Washington, D. C., 10, 14, 53
Watkins, James C., 94
Weeks, Doris Short, 85-86
West Florida, 6-7, 9-10, 13-14, 22, 49
Westcott, James D., Jr., 22, 24
Whidden, Vance, 85
Whigs, 25, 43
white primary, 88
Widden, John J., 45
Williams, Francis "Cowboy," 93, 95
Winstead, Ray, 96
World War I, 71
World War II, 70, 91

Z

Zimmerman, W. C., 28